THE WILD HISTORY OF THE AMERICAN WEST

THE TEXAS FIGHT
FOR INDEPENDENCE
—FROM THE ALAMO
TO SAN JACINTO

John Albert Torres

MyReportLinks.com Books
an imprint of

 Enslow Publishers, Inc.
Box 398, 40 Industrial Road
Berkeley Heights, NJ 07922
USA

MyReportLinks.com Books, an imprint of Enslow Publishers, Inc. MyReportLinks®
is a registered trademark of Enslow Publishers, Inc.

Library of Congress Cataloging-in-Publication Data

Torres, John Albert.
  The Texas fight for independence : from the Alamo to San Jacinto / John Albert Torres.
    p. cm. — (The wild history of the American West)
  Includes bibliographical references and index.
  ISBN 1-59845-011-5
  1. Texas—History—Revolution, 1835–1836—Juvenile literature. 2. Texas—
History—Revolution, 1835–1836—Biography—Juvenile literature. 3. Alamo (San
Antonio, Tex.)—Siege, 1836—Juvenile literature. I. Title. II. Series.
  F390.T69 2006
  976.4'03—dc22

2006000212

Printed in the United States of America

10 9 8 7 6 5 4 3 2 1

To Our Readers:
Through the purchase of this book, you and your library gain access to the Report Links that specifically
back up this book.
The Publisher will provide access to the Report Links that back up this book and will keep these Report
Links up to date on **www.myreportlinks.com** for five years from the book's first publication date.
We have done our best to make sure all Internet addresses in this book were active and appropriate when
we went to press. However, the author and the Publisher have no control over, and assume no liability
for, the material available on those Internet sites or on other Web sites they may link to.
The usage of the MyReportLinks.com Books Web site is subject to the terms and conditions stated on the
Usage Policy Statement on **www.myreportlinks.com.**
A password may be required to access the Report Links that back up this book. The password is found
on the bottom of page 4 of this book.
Any comments or suggestions can be sent by e-mail to comments@myreportlinks.com or to the address
on the back cover.

Photo Credits: Clipart.com, p. 57; © Corel Corporation, pp. 30–31, 61; © 1995 PhotoDisc, Inc, p. 3
(Alamo); © 1999 PhotoDisc, Inc., pp. 10–11; *Courtesy of Dictionary of American Portraits,* © 1967 by
Dover Publications, Inc., pp. 21, 68; Dallas Historical Society, pp. 25, 71; Daughters of the Republic of
Texas, Inc., pp. 18, 48; Donald J. Mabry/The Historical Text Archive, p. 40; Electronic Text Center:
University of Virginia Library, p. 65; Enslow Publishers, Inc., pp. 9, 85; Lamont Wood, p. 73; Library of
Congress, pp. 1, 3 (Houston head shot), 7 (dog and man panning for gold, Indian chief), 16, 26, 44, 51,
55, 70, 74–75, 96, 101, 106, 111, 114–115, 116; MyReportLinks.com Books, p. 4; National Center for
Public Policy Research, p. 89; National Park Service, p. 7 (train); PBS Online, p. 9; Photos.com, pp. 6, 7
(background, buffalo, wagon train); San Jacinto Museum of History, p. 98; Smithsonian National
Museum of American History, p. 113; Texas Council for the Humanities, p. 63; Texas Department of
Transportation, pp. 78–79; Texas State Historical Association, pp. 34, 42, 59, 81, 87, 93; Texas State
Library & Archives Commission, pp. 82–83, 94, 104, 108; The Avalon Project at Yale Law School, The
Lillian Goldman Law Library in Memory of Sol Goldman, p. 35; The Sam Houston Memorial Museum,
p. 20; The West Film Project and WETA, pp. 46, 52; University of Texas Libraries, pp. 5, 38; U.S. State
Department, p. 112; Virtual Field Trip Network, p. 23; Wallace L. McKeehan, pp. 28, 90, 102; Weider
History Group, p. 14.

Cover Illustration: Library of Congress

Cover Description: "Battle of the Alamo" by artist Percy Moran, created circa 1912.

CONTENTS

MyReportLinks.com Books
Great Books, Great Links, Great for Research!

The Internet sites featured in this book can save you hours of research time. These Internet sites—we call them *"Report Links"*—are constantly changing, but we keep them up to date on our Web site.

When you see this "Approved Web Site" logo, you will know that we are directing you to a great Internet site that will help you with your research.

Give it a try! Type http://www.myreportlinks.com into your browser, click on the series title and enter the password, then click on the book title, and scroll down to the Report Links listed for this book.

The Report Links will bring you to great source documents, photographs, and illustrations. MyReportLinks.com Books save you time, feature Report Links that are kept up to date, and make report writing easier than ever! A complete listing of the Report Links can be found on pages 118–119 at the back of the book.

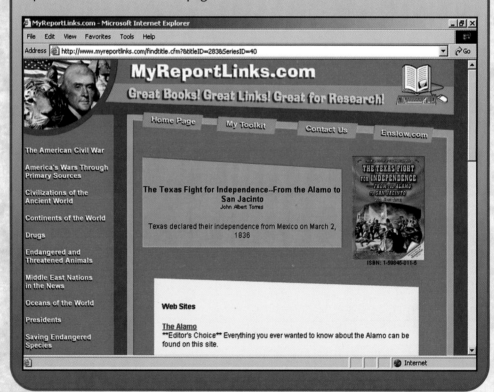

Please see "To Our Readers" on the copyright page for important information about this book, the MyReportLinks.com Web site, and the Report Links that back up this book.

Please enter WTF1265 if asked for a password.

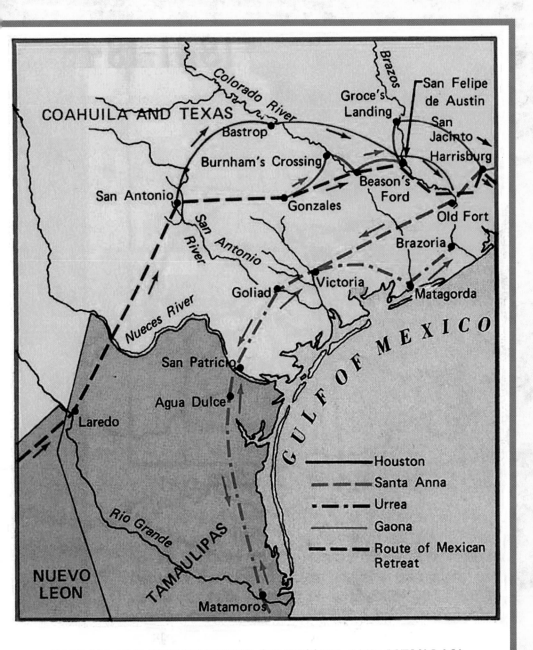

THE MAJOR MOVEMENTS OF TEXAN AND MEXICAN MILITARY FORCES, FEBRUARY– APRIL, 1836

1836 —*February 8:* Former congressman and popular frontiersman and soldier David Crockett arrives at the Alamo with a group of volunteers.

—*February 12:* Captain William Barret Travis is elected commander of the enlisted soldiers at the Alamo. At the same time, James Bowie is elected leader of the volunteer soldiers.

—*February 23:* General Antonio López de Santa Anna and his Mexican Army reach what is present-day San Antonio, Texas, where the Alamo is located.

—*March 1:* The forces at the Alamo are reinforced by thirty-two men who had come from the town of Gonzales.

—*March 2:* Texas Declaration of Independence is approved at a convention in Washington-on-the-Brazos.

—*March 6:* Mexican forces attack the Alamo. All defenders are killed. The only survivors are women, children, and a slave named Joe who belonged to Captain Travis. The number of Mexican soldiers killed is estimated to be 600. There is no accurate record of the number of Alamo defenders killed, but it is believed to be about 189.

—*March 20:* Troops led by Colonel James W. Fannin are captured after a battle near a town called Coleto.

—*March 27:* Fannin and his men are executed at a town named Goliad.

—*April 21:* The Texian Army soundly defeats Santa Anna's forces at the Battle of San Jacinto.

—*May 14:* Santa Anna signs the Treaties of Velasco, and Mexican troops retreat south of the Rio Grande.

—*September:* The Republic of Texas officially becomes an independent country after a constitution is approved. Sam Houston is elected the president of the Republic of Texas.

▷ **1837** —*February:* San Antonio officially becomes a town in Bexar County, Texas.

▷ **1840** —Austin is selected as the capital city of the Republic of Texas.

▷ **1845** —*December:* The Republic of Texas is annexed by the United States of America, becoming the twenty-eighth state on December 29.

▷ **1861** —*February:* Texas secedes from the United States and joins the Confederate States of America during the Civil War.

▷ **1865** —*May 12–13:* Final battle of the Civil War is fought near Brownsville, Texas, over a month after the Confederacy's top leader, General Robert E. Lee, surrendered at Appomattox Court House, Virginia.

A map of Texas. ▷

Chapter 1

THE ALAMO

The cannon were not yet firing, but they were ready.

The little old church, the Mission San Antonio de Valero, was eerily quiet on the morning of February 23, 1836. Though it had once been a place of worship, it had stopped being a religious place long before that day. The eighteen cannon

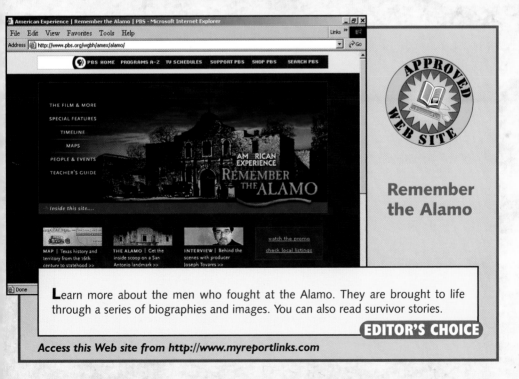

Learn more about the men who fought at the Alamo. They are brought to life through a series of biographies and images. You can also read survivor stories.

EDITOR'S CHOICE

Access this Web site from http://www.myreportlinks.com

The Alamo had been a Roman Catholic mission before the Texas freedom fighters used it as a fort.

on top of the walls and in gun placements had turned the tiny compound into a mini-fortress, dubbed the Alamo. In fact it was the highest concentration of cannon anywhere west of the great Mississippi River. For the most part, west of the river was a lot of uncharted territory. It is amazing to think that this tiny old Catholic mission was the best fort around.

Little did anyone at the Alamo know that events there would shape the futures of Mexico and Texas. Just a few years earlier, the Mexican government permitted Americans to come and settle in the land now known as Texas. There they had a chance to acquire plenty of cheap land that was perfect for raising cattle and farming. But now the Texians (American settlers living in Texas), wanted to break free of Mexican rule. Similarly to the American colonials' dispute with Great Britain, the Texians had no voice in government. They had no say on how things should be done. They were tired and frustrated. They were also upset that Mexican leader Santa Anna banned slavery. The Texians relied on slaves to work their large plantations and ranches.

It was here, at the dusty little old mission named the Alamo, that the fight for Texas independence would turn violent.

Colonel William Travis received word that the Mexican Army had been spotted miles away and was quickly approaching. At least two thousand seasoned Mexican soldiers approached the Alamo to squash a rebellion among the men and women of Texas who were tired of Mexican rule. They wanted to form a new republic—they wanted to be independent. Word was that another two thousand Mexican troops or more would soon be there as well.

There had been quite a few little battles here and there throughout Texas against the Mexican soldiers. Now the country's dictator, or ruler, General Antonio López de Santa Anna, was leading a massive force of soldiers and cannon into Texas. Santa Anna hoped to squash the revolution once and for all and go back to his lavish palace.

The almost two hundred soldiers and volunteers guarding the Alamo did not think the Mexican Army would arrive. They never expected any fighting to take place. Everyone knew about the hostility that existed between Mexico and the Texas settlers, but no one really expected that the tension would erupt into a war. The men of the Alamo were an older bunch, tired of fighting and just looking for a little peace and some land. When they saw the Mexicans they appeared dumbfounded. Many of them had never seen a real army before. Some of the volunteers, such as David "Davy" Crockett, were known more for

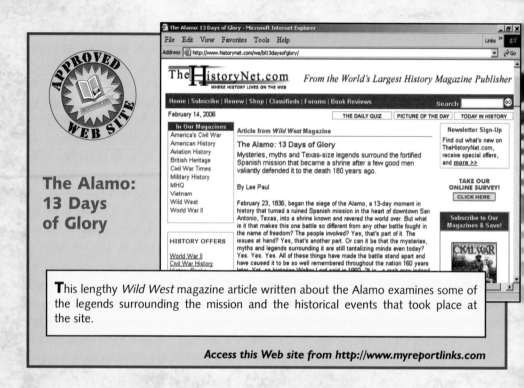

The Alamo:
13 Days
of Glory

The Alamo: 13 Days of Glory - Microsoft Internet Explorer

File   Edit   View   Favorites   Tools   Help

Address http://www.historynet.com/we/bl13daysofglory/

The HistoryNet.com   *From the World's Largest History Magazine Publisher*
WHERE HISTORY LIVES ON THE WEB

Home | Subscribe | Renew | Shop | Classifieds | Forums | Book Reviews   Search

February 14, 2006   THE DAILY QUIZ   PICTURE OF THE DAY   TODAY IN HISTORY

In Our Magazines
America's Civil War
American History
Aviation History
British Heritage
Civil War Times
Military History
MHQ
Vietnam
Wild West
World War II

Article from *Wild West* Magazine

The Alamo: 13 Days of Glory
Mysteries, myths and Texas-size legends surround the fortified
Spanish mission that became a shrine after a few good men
valiantly defended it to the death 180 years ago.

By Lee Paul

February 23, 1836, began the siege of the Alamo, a 13-day moment in
history that turned a ruined Spanish mission in the heart of downtown San
Antonio, Texas, into a shrine known and revered the world over. But what
is it that makes this one battle so different from any other battle fought in
the name of freedom? The people involved? Yes, that's part of it. The
issues at hand? Yes, that's another part. Or can it be that the mysteries,
myths and legends surrounding it are still tantalizing minds even today?
Yes. Yes. Yes. All of these things have made the battle stand apart and
have caused it to be so well remembered throughout the nation 160 years

HISTORY OFFERS
World War II
Civil War History

Newsletter Sign-Up
Find out what's new on
TheHistoryNet.com,
receive special offers,
and more >>

TAKE OUR
ONLINE SURVEY!
CLICK HERE

Subscribe to Our
Magazines & Save!

This lengthy *Wild West* magazine article written about the Alamo examines some of
the legends surrounding the mission and the historical events that took place at
the site.

Access this Web site from http://www.myreportlinks.com

hunting bear and exploring than fighting trained
and disciplined soldiers. The men at the Alamo
were, for the most part, family men who had
joined the militia in exchange for a piece of land
in Texas.

In fact, Crockett, who was already a legendary
figure in American history, had slowed down his
wild ways and had even spent a few years as a
United States congressman from Tennessee. When
he was voted out after his first term, he decided
to take up an offer from his friend Sam Houston.
He told the people of Tennessee, "Since you have
chosen to elect a man with a timber toe to suc-
ceed me, you may all go to hell and I will go to

Texas."[1] He told his wife, Elizabeth, he would settle in Texas "in hopes of making a fortune for my family, bad as has been my prospects."[2]

So Crockett, who was always looking for a new adventure, donned his famous coonskin cap and gathered a band of followers who would be very loyal to him. The group became known as Crockett and his volunteers. Crockett had no trouble living up to his legendary status; in fact, his bravery was one of the many inspirational stories to come out of the Alamo.

As the massive army approached and then made camp within firing range of the makeshift fort, one thing was clear: the men inside the Alamo had no chance and Santa Anna knew it.

The general, who was known to admire the famous European conqueror Napoléon, did not order an attack right away. Some believe Santa Anna was hoping Texas general Sam Houston would arrive with his army. Santa Anna then hoped he could crush Houston's army and win the war in one decisive battle.

When he learned that Houston was still many days away and was still trying to raise an army, Santa Anna decided to try and end this little skirmish without bloodshed. He sent a few riders holding the white flag of peace to ride toward the fort. Colonel William Travis sent some of his men along to see what the Mexicans wanted. Santa

Anna wanted the men of the Alamo to surrender. They would be taken prisoner and no one would get hurt. But what would that do for the Texians hopes for independence? Surely they would never be free of Santa Anna's iron fist.

The soldiers and volunteers looked to Crockett and to Jim Bowie, a great and fierce fighter the men respected, to tell them what to do. Bowie used to carry a large knife, almost like a small sword, that became known as the Bowie Knife.

One thing was clear. Nobody in the fort wanted to die. They had gone there to settle down to a life of open land and peace. But it was not up to Crockett, Bowie, or anybody else. Colonel William Travis was in command and it would be

This classic engraving of David Crockett shows him with his famous cap, three dogs, and a rifle.

his decision and his decision alone. But Travis was young and did not know the men very well. Many did not want him to be in charge. He did not think long of Santa Anna's order to surrender. He knew what response was needed if Texas was ever to be free.

He ordered a cannon fired at the Mexican Army. The men looked at him and were stunned. But that was his decision, so a cannon was fired. There would be no turning back now—there would be no peace.

What happened next must have sent a chill up the backs of everyone in the fort. Santa Anna raised a red flag over his encampment. This red flag meant that once the battle started, the Mexicans would take no prisoners. They would kill anyone who defended the fort against them.

Why did Travis do this? Why would he risk everyone's life in the tiny mission that was now surrounded by a massive force of soldiers? Historian Lamont Wood explains it simply:

> The Alamo teaches us that even if you're surrounded, outnumbered ten to one, they've announced they're taking no prisoners, and they're pouring over the walls, within your soul you have options. You can decide that something is worth dying for. That here is where you will stand. That here is where you will draw the line. Because there is such a thing as victory in death, there is such a thing as

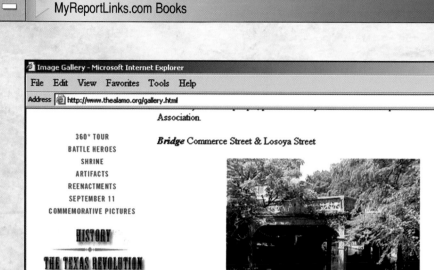

Texan and Mexican officials met on this bridge to discuss affairs before the Mexican Army attacked the Alamo. Learn more about this important battle and those who fought in it at **The Alamo** Web site.

immortality, if something is worth dying for, that means it is also worth living for.[3]

The Mexicans responded with cheers to the cannon shot. Then the bombardment began. The Mexicans slammed the fort's walls with cannon fire for several hours. Luckily for the soldiers and volunteers inside the Alamo, the Mexican Army was still waiting for their big cannon to arrive. Because they were so heavy and hard to transport, the large cannon were still a few days behind the soldiers. Once the cannon arrived, there would be no hope for those at the fort. The cannon meant that the Mexicans could pummel the walls of the Alamo with a nonstop barrage before anyone at the Alamo could reach them with a rifle or cannon shot of their own.

For now, the Mexicans would have to fire back with little cannon. This artillery did some damage to the fort but not much. The cannon fire was really meant to scare or intimidate the soldiers and volunteers inside the fort. After the cannon fire started, Travis went to his office to write a letter. His men did not fire back. The Mexicans were still out of range and the men inside the Alamo would have to save as much of their ammunition and supplies as they could. The document, a plea for help, has become known as Travis's Appeal.

The letter was sent by two messengers to all parts of Texas, especially to anyone who had an army or militia, including General Sam Houston. Travis made it clear that he was willing to die for the cause of Texas, but he also wanted people to know that his men were on the verge of being massacred.

"I am besieged with a thousand or more of the Mexicans under Santa Anna," the appeal starts. "I have sustained a continual bombardment and cannonade for 24 hours and have not lost a man. The enemy has demanded a surrender at discretion;

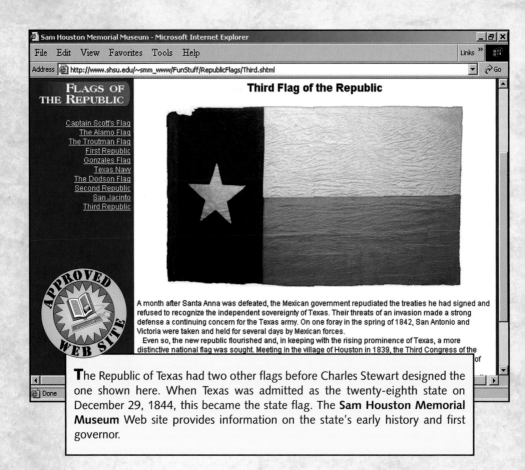

Sam Houston Memorial Museum - Microsoft Internet Explorer

File   Edit   View   Favorites   Tools   Help   Links »

Address http://www.shsu.edu/~smm_www/FunStuff/RepublicFlags/Third.shtml   Go

FLAGS OF THE REPUBLIC

Captain Scott's Flag
The Alamo Flag
The Troutman Flag
First Republic
Gonzales Flag
Texas Navy
The Dodson Flag
Second Republic
San Jacinto
Third Republic

Third Flag of the Republic

A month after Santa Anna was defeated, the Mexican government repudiated the treaties he had signed and refused to recognize the independent sovereignty of Texas. Their threats of an invasion made a strong defense a continuing concern for the Texas army. On one foray in the spring of 1842, San Antonio and Victoria were taken and held for several days by Mexican forces.

Even so, the new republic flourished and, in keeping with the rising prominence of Texas, a more distinctive national flag was sought. Meeting in the village of Houston in 1839, the Third Congress of the

The Republic of Texas had two other flags before Charles Stewart designed the one shown here. When Texas was admitted as the twenty-eighth state on December 29, 1844, this became the state flag. The **Sam Houston Memorial Museum** Web site provides information on the state's early history and first governor.

otherwise the garrison is to be put to the sword, if the fort is taken. Have answered the demand with a cannon shot and our flag still waves proudly over the wall. I shall never surrender or retreat. Then I call on you in the name of liberty, of patriotism, of everything dear to the American character, to come to our aid with all dispatch. The enemy is receiving reinforcements daily and will no doubt increase to three or four thousand in four or five days. If this call is neglected I am determined to sustain myself as long as possible and die like a soldier who never

▲ Captain William Barret Travis is said to have drawn a line in the sand to inspire his men to fight to the death.

forgets what is due his honor and that of his country. Victory or death."[4]

The cannon shot and the dramatic and desperate appeal for help would only be surpassed in high drama by another gesture Travis made over the next few days. After it was clear that no help would arrive in time and that the Mexicans were bent on destroying not only the fort but the spirit of Texas independence, Travis gave the men of the Alamo a chance to leave the fort safely.

As legend has it, he called a meeting among everyone in the fort and in simple terms explained to them that no help would be coming. He explained to them what was at stake and that they would be needed to sacrifice their lives in order to buy Sam Houston more time to get an army together. He did not mince words. He was clear and direct.

With his sword he then supposedly drew a line in the sand. He said anyone that was willing to fight and die with him at the Alamo should cross the line and stand with him. Everyone did except for one man.

His name was Louis Rose, a fifty-year-old Frenchman, whom everyone called "Moses" because of his age. Rose had the reputation as a fierce warrior and a lifelong soldier who had fought in Napoléon's army in France and in Russia. Rose had accompanied Napoléon when he

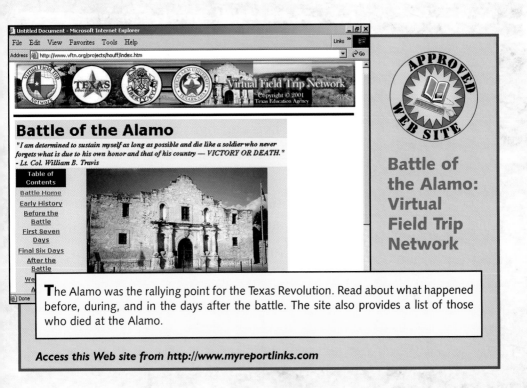

Battle of the Alamo: Virtual Field Trip Network

The Alamo was the rallying point for the Texas Revolution. Read about what happened before, during, and in the days after the battle. The site also provides a list of those who died at the Alamo.

Access this Web site from http://www.myreportlinks.com

invaded Russia in June 1812. He witnessed first-hand the horrors of a terrible defeat when Napoléon's army was decimated.

Years later, he found himself in the New World and fighting for Texas independence. He was a rifleman under the command of James Bowie and he had participated in many of the brutal skirmishes that took place against the Mexicans before the Battle of the Alamo took place. But as he took his position every day and night on the Alamo's walls, he took notice of the growing size of Santa Anna's forces. He saw the cannon being moved closer and closer by the day. He knew that everyone in the Alamo would die. They stood no chance against the enemy forces.

Rose chose to leave the Alamo. Some considered him to be a coward. Others thought he was smart to survive to live and fight another day. He died fifteen years later, working as a butcher in Louisiana.

Up until the moment when Travis drew a line in the sand, the men of the Alamo had kept their spirits high by playing music and games at night. But now, things had been spelled out and the seriousness of the situation made clear. But another remarkable thing had happened in those few days. Travis had earned their respect at last. Roughly two hundred soldiers and volunteers were willing to die alongside of him.

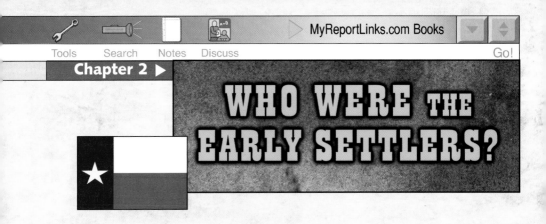

Chapter 2 ▶

WHO WERE THE EARLY SETTLERS?

Before Spanish and other European explorers and settlers came to the area known as Texas or Mexico, those lands were filled with American Indians. The European and American settlers came and brought a new culture and goods from foreign lands. They also brought new diseases to the natives. The American Indians were not

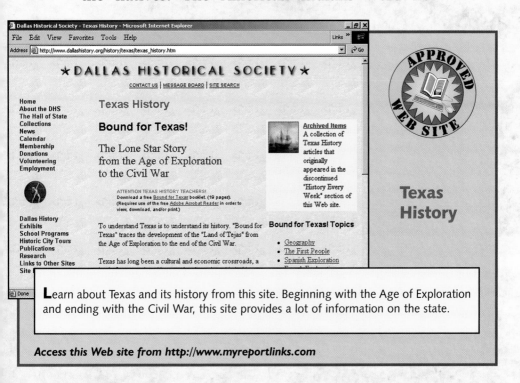

Learn about Texas and its history from this site. Beginning with the Age of Exploration and ending with the Civil War, this site provides a lot of information on the state.

Access this Web site from http://www.myreportlinks.com

△ *The Comanche were one of the major American Indian nations living in the Texas area. This photo of Chief Quanah Parker was taken between 1909 and 1932.*

immune to these new diseases and so the diseases became epidemic. That is, they spread rapidly and the effects were very serious. According to historians, 95 percent of the American Indians who lived in the Texas area were killed by the spread of European diseases.

Between 1629 and 1654 there were numerous Spanish explorations into the area known as Mexico. They soon started building Spanish missions that would serve two purposes. The missions would help the Catholic Church convert the American Indians who survived the epidemics and they would provide protection from the French who were also looking to expand their empire.

▷ New Spain

Texas had long been a colony of Spain. And as was customary of Spanish policy, they did not allow foreigners to settle in their lands. For many years the Spanish government—mainly the monarchy—tried to persuade its citizens to move to its territory and establish Mexico as a European-style country. They had an especially hard time trying to convince Spaniards to move to Texas. The land was remote and seemed isolated from other parts of Mexico.

So, in 1820, just before Mexico gained its independence from Spain, the Spanish government opened up Texas to American settlement. The tactic had worked once before for the Spanish when the European power owned the Louisiana Territory. The country encouraged Americans— or Anglos—to move to Louisiana, swear allegiance to the Spanish crown, become Spanish citizens, and convert to Catholicism. In exchange, they would be given generous land grants. But soon after allowing foreigners into Texas, Mexico earned its independence from the Spanish crown.

▷ Mexican Control

Mexico decided to continue with Spain's program of allowing foreigners into Texas. At that time there were only three established settlements in

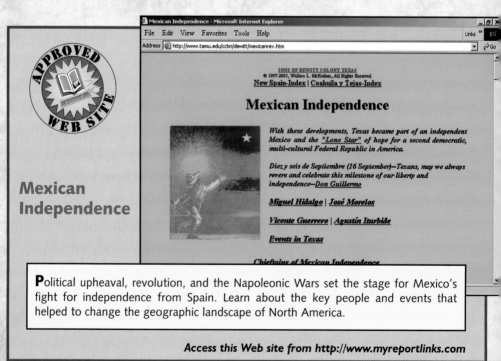

Mexican Independence

Political upheaval, revolution, and the Napoleonic Wars set the stage for Mexico's fight for independence from Spain. Learn about the key people and events that helped to change the geographic landscape of North America.

Access this Web site from http://www.myreportlinks.com

all of Texas. They were: Nacogdoches San Antonio de Béxar, and La Bahía del Espíritu Santo.

Moving to Texas was an attractive proposition for anyone who wanted to own land. For example, at this time—1821—100 acres of undeveloped land in the United States sold for about $100, which was payable at the time of the sale as long as someone was willing to buy 640 acres. Those willing to move their families to Texas and swear allegiance to another country were able to purchase 4,605 acres of land for $184! And they could pay that total off over six years.

Why They Came

There were other reasons for Americans to move to Texas in addition to cheap land. Many people believed that the United States would eventually purchase the eastern part of Texas—the part closest to Louisiana—from Mexico. They never dreamed that it would take a bloody revolution for the people of Texas to gain independence from Mexico.

Other people thought that eastern Texas was given to Mexico by the United States in exchange for Florida. The Texas pioneers were sure that the United States would own Texas soon and that they could resell their land at American prices and make fortunes.

TRA

David Crockett was one of the men who left his former life behind to seek prosperity in Texas. He ended up fighting alongside the men at the Alamo. His statue is the one to the right of the image. The Alamo Cenotaph that this statue is a part of is located in front of The Alamo in San Antonio, Texas.

JOSEPH KERR · GEORGE

CROCKETT

LE · WILLIAM P. KING · JOHN G. KING · WILLIAM IRVINE LEW
TION · THOMAS R. MILLER · WILLIAM MILLS · ISAAC M
JUAN ANTONIO PADILLO · WILLIAM PAR
A C. SMITH · WILLI

Mexico—or the Texas region of Mexico—was also attractive to people who owed a lot of money or who were perhaps in trouble with the law. There was no extradition treaty between Mexico and the United States. This means that if someone committed a crime in the United States, Mexico was not obligated to return that person to American police.

But despite swearing allegiance to Mexico and despite claiming to convert to Catholicism, many of the new settlers remained loyal to the United States and continued practicing their protestant religion.

New Lease on Life

Texas was a chance for many people to start over. After the War of 1812 ended, many American farmers in the Mississippi Valley went broke because of dropping prices for their crops. They could not pay loans back to banks, so many escaped to Mexico so they would not have to go to debtor's prison. And even though Mexico hated the notion of slavery, they allowed Texans who already owned slaves to bring them into Texas with them.

One man who wanted to start over was Moses Austin. He was an American who became a Spanish citizen in Louisiana and lost a lot of his money during the Panic of 1819. He applied to the Spanish government in 1820 for an empresario grant. The Mexican government would grant him land he could sell it for a still-bargain price of twelve cents an acre. Austin died in the middle of his plan. His son, Stephen Austin, took over the grant and brought three hundred families from Louisiana to settle in Texas. Of the original three hundred settlers, many were of British ancestry and very educated. In fact, only four of the three hundred could not read, according to historians. Stephen Austin would later play a pivotal role in the battle for Texas independence.

▷ Andrew Robinson

Another entrepreneur was a man named Andrew Robinson. Like Austin, the Spanish citizen applied for an empresario grant from the Mexican government and brought three hundred families with him to an area in the town of Washington known as Washington-on-the-Brazos. The area used to be known as Washington but it was very close to the Brazos River and so the name was changed. Robinson was a man of vision and he had a plan for a town to grow in the area that became Washington-on-the-Brazos. He started a ferry service so that people could easily cross the river.

Because of this ferry service, commerce thrived and businessmen began flocking to the town to open businesses and factories. The town was actually in a perfect location. It was elevated, so it was

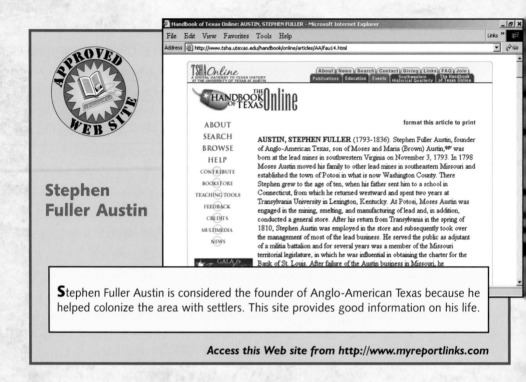

Stephen Fuller Austin

APPROVED WEB SITE

Stephen Fuller Austin is considered the founder of Anglo-American Texas because he helped colonize the area with settlers. This site provides good information on his life.

Access this Web site from http://www.myreportlinks.com

not prone to flooding and there was plenty of fresh water available. It became a popular place and soon was populated with mainly Americans who began talking of independence from Mexico.

▷ Cause for Revolution

The reason that talk of independence began to sprout up was because the people of Texas felt they had been ignored when the new government of Mexico devised its Centralist Constitution. The people of Texas had few rights under the new laws and little representation in government. Also, the new constitution called for the end of slavery— something that the Anglo colonists counted on.

It is interesting to note that people's diets consisted mainly of pork and corn. People ate cornbread, hominy, and tortillas, according to John Lienhard of the University of Houston. Green vegetables, such as lettuce, were rarely eaten, and beef was never eaten because livestock was considered too valuable.

Publicly, the United States remained neutral in whatever disagreements there were between Mexico and the Texas settlers. Yet there was considerable support for the settlers from other Americans in the form of money, guns, and volunteers. Secretly, the Americans were funding the independence movement against Mexico.

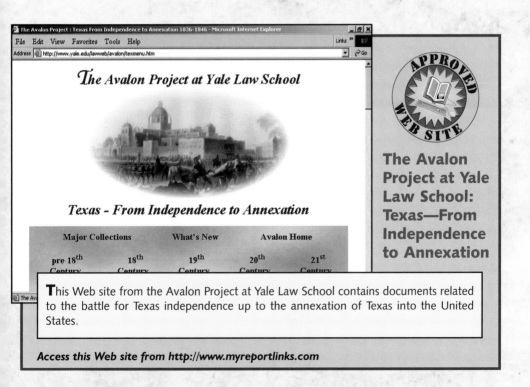

The Avalon Project at Yale Law School: Texas—From Independence to Annexation

This Web site from the Avalon Project at Yale Law School contains documents related to the battle for Texas independence up to the annexation of Texas into the United States.

Access this Web site from http://www.myreportlinks.com

Ten years after Robinson started the town, it became the center of revolution against Mexico. In fact, General Sam Houston made it his headquarters, and in 1836, delegates of the Texas signed a declaration of independence.

Part of that declaration, which was patterned after the U.S. Declaration of Independence, called for the area of Texas to be annexed into the United States. But President Andrew Jackson declined, knowing it would mean that the United States would have to go to war with Mexico. Also, he knew that many of the northern states would not allow another pro-slavery state into the union.

No, gaining Texas independence would not be as easy as making a simple declaration.

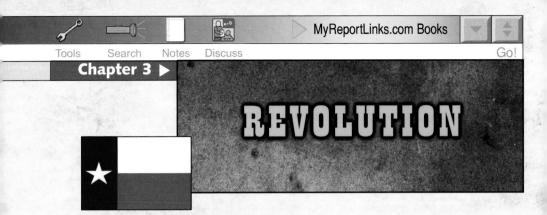

Chapter 3

REVOLUTION

The Battle of the Alamo started years before anyone outside of Texas ever heard of that little Spanish mission known as the Alamo. Like most struggles for freedom, the Battle of the Alamo and the struggle for Texas independence began as a reaction to tyranny.

Tyranny is when a government keeps its people oppressed, or without rights. Mexico was a Spanish colony and Spain was ruled by a king. At that time, many people still believed that kings received their right to rule from God. The idea that all men are created equal, however, was starting to spread. This idea is the foundation for American democracy. It was a strange new idea, considered radical by many. On some places of the globe that way of thinking was considered revolutionary, and revolution began to spread.

▷ Independent From Europe

Decades earlier, the American colonies defeated the British Army to win American independence. Inspired by the Americans, the oppressed French

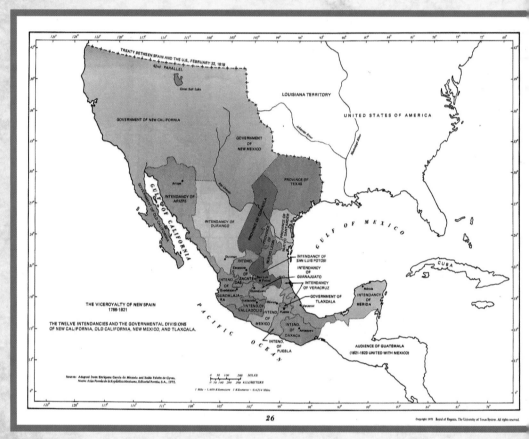

This is a map of New Spain showing the borders from 1786–1821. Most of New Spain eventually became Mexico.

people rose up and revolted against centuries of being ruled by a king.

Mexicans did not capitalize instantly on the revolutions going on around the world. Mexico was made up of many different peoples. Many of these people had been rival American Indian nations, and it would take awhile before people saw themselves as Mexicans rather than members of a different nation. Even still, many began to wonder if being ruled by a king so far away was a very good idea. Plus, the Spaniards, even those living in Mexico, did not treat the Mexicans well. Soon, they did not even treat their own people very well.

▷ Creoles and Gachupines

Spaniards who were born in Mexico, known as Creole, were treated badly by those born in Spain. The government also favored those born in Spain, known as Gachupines. They got the best pieces of land, the best jobs, and the best military appointments. Even if there were native Mexicans who worked harder or who were next in line for these lands or positions, they were passed over. If you were born in Spain, you were privileged.

Those born in Mexico, even those that considered themselves Spaniards, were not happy. They did not think it was fair. The seeds of revolution were now being planted.

Then something unexpected happened that would accelerate revolution throughout Mexico. Napoléon Bonaparte, the famous French Army general, invaded Spain in 1808. The brash military leader made his brother the new king of Spain. With Spaniards in Mexico now cut off from their homeland, the time was right for revolution.

▷ Miguel Hidalgo

With all that in place, the revolution still had an unlikely start. On September 16, 1810, a Catholic priest by the name of Father Miguel Hidalgo told his congregation the time had come. He was tired of seeing the privileged rich take advantage of the poor God-fearing people who sought refuge in the

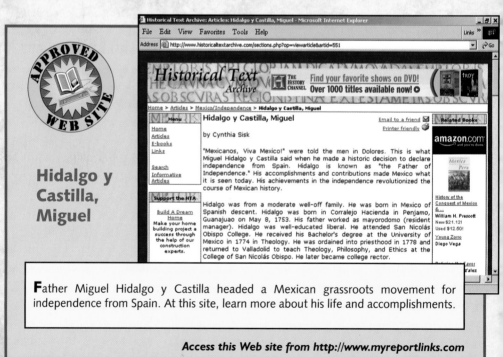

Hidalgo y Castilla, Miguel

Father Miguel Hidalgo y Castilla headed a Mexican grassroots movement for independence from Spain. At this site, learn more about his life and accomplishments.

Access this Web site from http://www.myreportlinks.com

church. He felt it was time for someone to speak up and against the tyranny that Mexicans had suffered so long at the hands of the Spaniards.

People everywhere were tired of being oppressed. Hidalgo told his congregation of peasants that rising up in revolution against Spanish officials would be the right thing to do. The revolution did not start in a giant open battlefield or with the firing of a cannon, it started in a small poor church filled with farmers whose families did not have enough to eat.

"His followers were predominantly peasants who saw the war as a way to gain land and punish their Spanish oppressors," writes Richard Bruce Winders, historian and curator of the Alamo.[1]

▷ A Violent Struggle

The first few battles were bloody and brutal. The peasants basically slaughtered whatever Spanish soldiers they came across. It was not quite what Hidalgo had envisioned. In fact, some say that he underestimated just how vicious and without mercy the peasants would be once they engaged in violent confrontations. This revolution, if it were to last, would not be easy and it would come at the price of many, many lives.

Eventually Hidalgo was caught and executed. That, however, could not stop the revolution.

Word of the insurgency spread quickly and soon armed rebels made their way into the vast mountains of Mexico.

▷ New Regime in Spain

Spaniards living in Spain decided to form a new government that was similar in nature to the one they always had. But there was one major difference that would change the shape of both Europe and North America for decades to come. The new government would not recognize the king of Spain as its leader. There might still be a king, but the real power would come from the people and the officials that represented them.

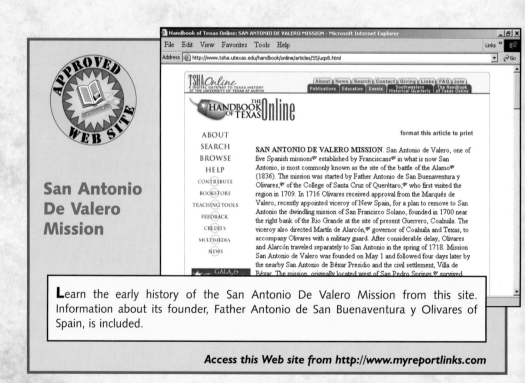

San Antonio De Valero Mission

Learn the early history of the San Antonio De Valero Mission from this site. Information about its founder, Father Antonio de san Buenaventura y Olivares of Spain, is included.

Access this Web site from http://www.myreportlinks.com

This was the chance that the Mexicans had been waiting for. This was the time for a revolution that had good chance of succeeding.

Having to deal with dramatic changes in its own country, Spain cared little for the goings on in Mexico. This further fueled the peasant-led revolution that was growing stronger every day. The first thing the native Mexicans did was to remove the Spaniards and Gachupines from government and any place of power and authority. A new Mexican government was formed and much of it was based on American and French beliefs that all men are created equal. The new plan contained one major flaw. Strangely enough, instead of forming a true republic—one in which the people had ultimate say over who ruled—they wanted to have an emperor or king. And since everyone believed that kings and emperors came from European families, the plan counted on a European nobleman coming to Mexico to claim the throne and lead the government. Remember, there were still many people in the world who felt that kings and emperors were chosen by God, so this was a very important part of this new government. But it turned out to be a huge mistake.

Iturbide

No one came forward and the country, ready with a new government, was rudderless—without a

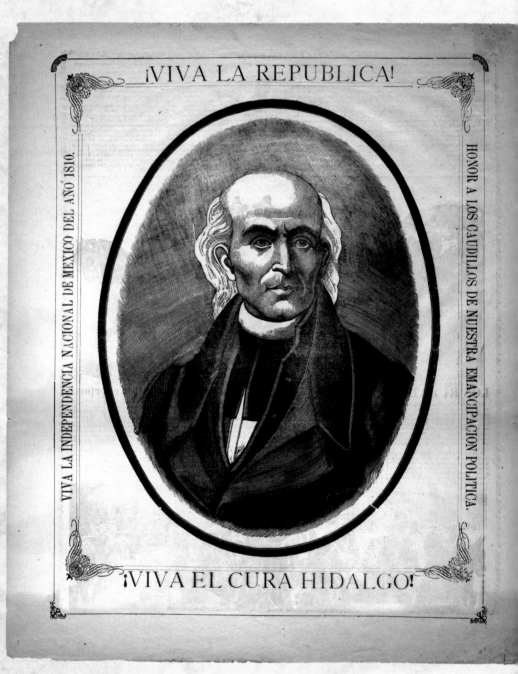

¡VIVA LA REPUBLICA!

VIVA LA INDEPENDENCIA NACIONAL DE MEXICO DEL AÑO 1810.

HONOR A LOS CAUDILLOS DE NUESTRA EMANCIPACION POLITICA.

¡VIVA EL CURA HIDALGO!

Father Miguel Hidalgo led a revolution in Mexico that helped bring about Mexican independence.

leader. This is when things began to sour. Revolutionary colonel Agustín de Iturbide claimed the throne. Right away there were people that did not think he should have that position because he was not a nobleman and he was not chosen by God.

And while he may have been a good soldier and a good revolutionary, he did not know how to govern people and was soon ousted. Mexicans then decided to form a government that was closer to the American government to their north.

Federal Constitution of 1824

Much like the United States, Mexico is a huge country. Many times, people who live in the southern most part of the country will not have the same interests or concerns as people who live in other parts of the country—like Texas, for example. The new government decided to divide the large country into eighteen states that would work together. This seemed to make the people more content. They felt as if they had a say in the federal government and their interests would be looked out for. This new agreement that broke the country up into various states was the Federal Constitution of 1824.

"Each state was free to adopt its own constitution as long as it did not conflict with the federal document," Winders writes.[2]

Mexico did not enjoy the success that the young American republic had. Presidents came and went before an era of military takeovers started. Whoever had control of the biggest army would challenge leadership and take over.

▷ Santa Anna

When General Antonio López de Santa Anna took control, he basically said that he would replace the Constitution of 1824. He did this as a way of consolidating his power.

That did not sit well with many Mexicans, especially those living in an area known as Texas. For years, Spaniards had been encouraging Americans to settle in Texas. They did not want this border

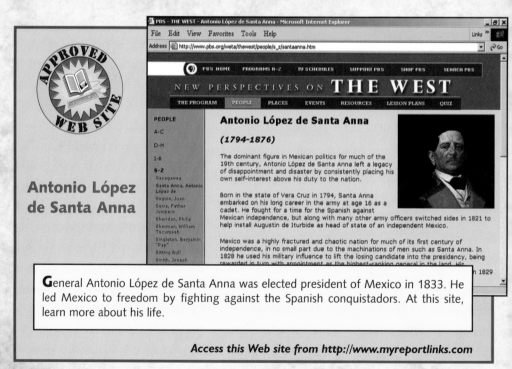

Antonio López de Santa Anna

PBS - THE WEST - Antonio López de Santa Anna - Microsoft Internet Explorer

File Edit View Favorites Tools Help   Links »

Address http://www.pbs.org/weta/thewest/people/s_z/santaanna.htm   Go

PBS HOME   PROGRAMS A-Z   TV SCHEDULES   SUPPORT PBS   SHOP PBS   SEARCH PBS

NEW PERSPECTIVES ON **THE WEST**

THE PROGRAM   PEOPLE   PLACES   EVENTS   RESOURCES   LESSON PLANS   QUIZ

PEOPLE

A-C

D-H

I-R

S-Z

Sacagawea

Santa Anna, Antonio López de

Seguín, Juan

Serra, Father Juniparo

Sheridan, Philip

Sherman, William Tecumseh

Singleton, Benjamin "Pap"

Sitting Bull

Smith, Joseph

Antonio López de Santa Anna

(1794-1876)

The dominant figure in Mexican politics for much of the 19th century, Antonio López de Santa Anna left a legacy of disappointment and disaster by consistently placing his own self-interest above his duty to the nation.

Born in the state of Vera Cruz in 1794, Santa Anna embarked on his long career in the army at age 16 as a cadet. He fought for a time for the Spanish against Mexican independence, but along with many other army officers switched sides in 1821 to help install Augustin de Iturbide as head of state of an independent Mexico.

Mexico was a highly fractured and chaotic nation for much of its first century of independence, in no small part due to the machinations of men such as Santa Anna. In 1828 he used his military influence to lift the losing candidate into the presidency, being rewarded in turn with appointment as the highest-ranking general in the land. His

n 1829

General Antonio López de Santa Anna was elected president of Mexico in 1833. He led Mexico to freedom by fighting against the Spanish conquistadors. At this site, learn more about his life.

Access this Web site from http://www.myreportlinks.com

area between Mexico and the United States to go unpopulated. They feared that another country might try and claim it—namely the French who had already taken over the area known as Louisiana. Most conflicts or wars between countries are over border areas just like this one.

In 1828, the government of Mexico sent officials to Texas to report on the population. There were some worries that the area was becoming too Americanized. Hoping to keep Texas as part of Mexico, the government passed a law in 1830 that prohibited any more Americans from moving into the Texas region. To prove that they were in charge, the Mexican government also decided to open tax offices throughout Texas and started building several forts. Things began to get much more restrictive on these settlers who were looking for freedom and open spaces to live in.

▷ Discontent

Many of the Americans living in the land known as Texas resented the changes and did not like living under these new stricter rules. In fact, many of them had moved out of the United States and into Texas because they wanted less government in their lives.

The Mexican government was ignoring history and making the same mistake that the Spaniards had made decades earlier. They were ruling the people with little regard for the people themselves. Once again, as in the time of Father Hidalgo, the people were being subjected to tyranny.

It was not just the Americans who felt this way. There was a certain freedom enjoyed by everyone who lived in this area. The tejanos enjoyed trading with Americans and had started looking at the federal republic in the United States as a government that had weathered challenges and was starting to work very well. It seemed like a better form of government than the one in Mexico.

Soon there was talk of a revolution and independence in an area where the people had always been happy being part of Mexico—that is, until the 1830 changes. A movement was underway

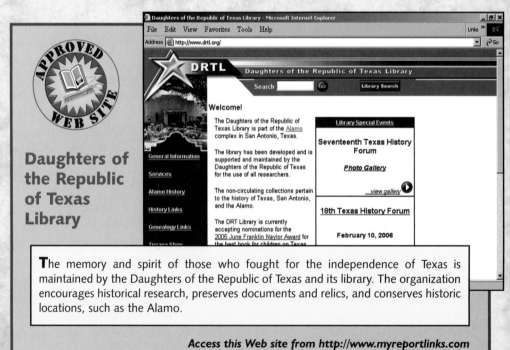

Daughters of the Republic of Texas Library

The memory and spirit of those who fought for the independence of Texas is maintained by the Daughters of the Republic of Texas and its library. The organization encourages historical research, preserves documents and relics, and conserves historic locations, such as the Alamo.

Access this Web site from http://www.myreportlinks.com

to make Texas an independent state—its own country. The idea, of course, was to try and accomplish this in a peaceful manner without any bloodshed. But the realists knew right away that Mexico would not let any of its territory become independent or fall into the hands of another country without a struggle.

▷ Start of an Uprising

If the tejanos and Texians were seriously thinking of challenging the massive army led by General Santa Anna, an army would have to rise from the streets themselves. The people, normal everyday people, would have to take up arms and form an army. And just like that first rebellion inspired by Father Hidalgo against the Spaniards, the people knew that there would be a steep price to pay for freedom from Mexico.

Even before all that, they would need a leader. There were only a few men who came to mind. They were different in nature and personality but both had a strong military background and just might be able to inspire an army or, in this case, rouse a volunteer army. The men were Sam Houston and Stephen Austin.

THE PEOPLE

Sam Houston was a war hero because after being wounded in battle, he won the respect of one of America's most decorated, courageous, and feared military leaders, Andrew Jackson. In 1814, Houston was badly injured and was expected to die in battle. Jackson watched as Houston lived and fought bravely. Houston's heroics made him extremely popular. Like many other former military leaders, he decided to enter the world of politics.

▷ Sam Houston

Sam Houston was born in 1793 to a military family in Virginia. But he spent almost all of his time hunting and exploring in the mountains of Tennessee. It was in these mountains that he befriended the Cherokee Indians. Houston chose to live among the Indians for some time before coming back from the wilderness with the desire to open his own law practice.

Houston became an attorney and also enlisted as a soldier when the War of 1812 broke out. After

▲ Andrew Jackson was a decorated war general and one of the most well-known presidents of the United States. Jackson was impressed with Sam Houston's bravery when they had fought together.

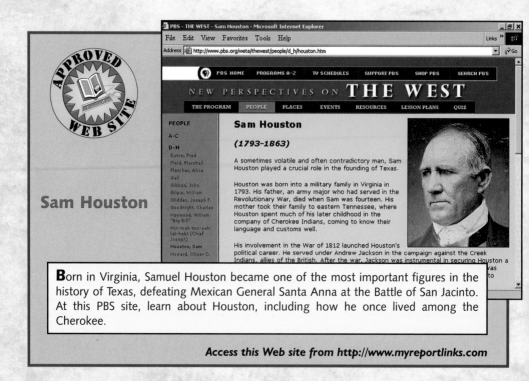

Sam Houston

Sam Houston

(1793-1863)

A sometimes volatile and often contradictory man, Sam Houston played a crucial role in the founding of Texas.

Houston was born into a military family in Virginia in 1793. His father, an army major who had served in the Revolutionary War, died when Sam was fourteen. His mother took their family to eastern Tennessee, where Houston spent much of his later childhood in the company of Cherokee Indians, coming to know their language and customs well.

His involvement in the War of 1812 launched Houston's political career. He served under Andrew Jackson in the campaign against the Creek Indians, allies of the British. After the war, Jackson was instrumental in securing Houston a

Born in Virginia, Samuel Houston became one of the most important figures in the history of Texas, defeating Mexican General Santa Anna at the Battle of San Jacinto. At this PBS site, learn about Houston, including how he once lived among the Cherokee.

Access this Web site from http://www.myreportlinks.com

nearly dying from three mortal wounds at the Battle of Horseshoe Bend, Houston took up politics. He was elected to the U.S. Congress in 1823 and then reelected in 1825. In 1827, he was elected governor of Tennessee. A few years later he would find himself in Texas.

▷ Stephen Austin

Stephen Austin was the other hope for the people of the Texas region. He had lived in a Mexican prison for quite some time and in fact, already commanded a battalion of five companies when the Mexican government made him a lieutenant colonel years before.

If the battle for Texas independence was indeed going to be won and lost on a battlefield, then Austin and Houston had a tough opponent facing them. General Santa Anna had a long history of backing the right side and influencing the people needed to help keep him in power and his army going strong.

A Strong Foe

He was one of the army's main fighters and leaders who helped crush Father Hidalgo's revolt against the Spaniards in 1810. Then, in 1829 he was part of the rebel army that helped crush those same Spanish officials he had once protected. Like many, he felt those Spanish leaders had kept the Mexican people down for too long. He proudly patterned his military strategy after the European style of fighting, and in particular, the strategies of Napoléon.

But before meeting on a battlefield or clearing the dead away from a fort, the colonists, which residents of Texas were now calling themselves, still held out hope that they could achieve independence in a peaceful manner. In April 1833, the colonists came together and asked Austin if he would go to the country's capital, Mexico City, and ask the government of Mexico to grant them independence. Even Austin thought that might be asking for too much. He carried with him a petition that included a new constitution for Mexico that did not include Texas. Stephen Austin asked all of his friends in politics to help him try and sway the government. But their pleas fell on deaf ears. The government said no to Texas statehood. No one was really surprised because land was the Mexican governments only asset.

Even though Austin knew they would say no, he was upset and his resolve—his hope—for independence was even stronger than ever. He wrote a letter to the colonists in Texas and told them the time had had come for independence. He told them to get ready for statehood.

But government officials read a copy of the very strong letter and became worried. They felt that Austin had gone too far and was now openly inciting revolution. Government soldiers arrested him and kept in prison for about a year.

▷ Santa Anna and Austin

When he was released, Austin immediately went back home to Texas. More than ever he was convinced that Texas had to act aggressively if it was ever going to be free from the Mexican government. Oddly enough, Santa Anna authorized Austin's release. He thought Austin could calm the Texans down and sway them away from their dreams of independence.

At one time, Mexican leader Santa Anna and Stephen Austin had been allies. At first, Santa Anna thought Austin could help him settle the problems the Texians had with the Mexican government.

Austin was born in 1793 in Virginia and raised in Southeast Missouri. A very good student, he was enrolled at Connecticut's Yale College (now Yale University) when he was eleven years old.

In 1813, when he was twenty-one years old, he was elected to the Missouri Legislature and reelected every year until 1819 when he moved to Arkansas. He worked at a variety of careers including storekeeper, bank manager, and running the family's lead mining business.

Meanwhile, his father, Moses, obtained a grant for land to introduce a colony of Americans to Texas. But he died before his dream became realized and so it fell to his son to accomplish. Stephen Austin moved to Texas and worked for years to fulfill his father's wishes.

▷ Santa Anna Calls on a Peacemaker

During this time the Mexican Army was already involved in several revolts around the country. They were trying to crush a federalist movement that was sprouting up around the country. Santa Anna was leading the army and he had no problem in making an example of those who dared defy the government.

Austin gained a strong reputation as a peacemaker and someone who prevented violence as long as there was a chance for peace. He later became known as the Father of Texas.

▲ This antique cannon is on display at The Alamo. Cannon played a big part in each battle of the conflict between the Texans and the Mexican Army.

Battle of Gonzales

The revolts and skirmishes were coming closer and closer to Texas, including one small battle where colonists refused to give a cannon back to the Mexican Army. This came to be known as the Battle of Gonzales. Instead, they fired the cannon on the Mexicans themselves. Finally, the Mexican government sent a small garrison to Texas to start collecting more taxes on goods entering Texas from the United States. That did it, the Texans had had enough. William B. Travis rounded up a group of volunteers to march against these Mexican soldiers. They defeated the Mexicans and made them retreat.

William Barret Travis

William Barret Travis would emerge as one of the key figures in the defending of the Alamo and the push for Texas independence. Travis was born in 1809, the eldest of eleven children, in South Carolina. The family owned a small farm, and Travis later owned some land in Texas. Travis was always active with his studies, working on the family farm or taking part in some activity at the Red Bank Church.

Travis's concentration on his studies really increased starting in 1817 when his family moved to Alabama. Travis became a teacher, then a lawyer, and opened his own law practice. When he turned twenty, Travis was a successful lawyer. He married one of his students, and it seemed as if he would lead a quiet and prosperous life.

He became the publisher of the town newspaper and joined a Masonic lodge. It looked as though Travis planned on spending his life in the town of Claiborne, Alabama.

Then something odd happened. One year later, Travis picked up his belongings and abandoned his wife (Rosanna Cato Travis), child, and unborn child to move to Texas. He also left behind a very successful law practice.

No one knows for sure why Travis left his thriving law practice, pregnant wife, and young child

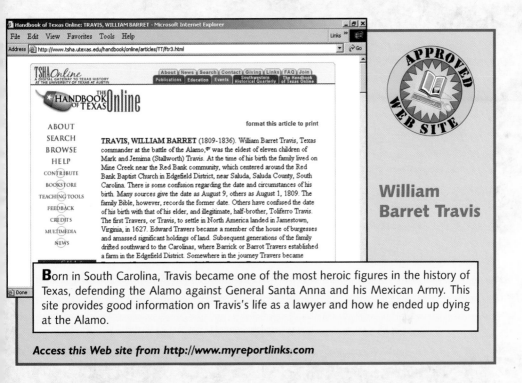

William Barret Travis

Born in South Carolina, Travis became one of the most heroic figures in the history of Texas, defending the Alamo against General Santa Anna and his Mexican Army. This site provides good information on Travis's life as a lawyer and how he ended up dying at the Alamo.

Access this Web site from http://www.myreportlinks.com

back home in Alabama to start over, but many speculate that Travis's wife had been unfaithful to him and that he even may have killed the man he suspected of being her lover. Historians agree that this is likely although there is no clear documentation or solid evidence to back the claim.

When he arrived in Texas, Travis fell in with a very vocal pro-independence group of people and soon shared their feelings. His wife demanded a divorce, and one of Travis's friends went and brought Travis his son. Travis agreed to the divorce, and she remarried almost immediately.

He would later find himself the unexpected leader of anywhere from 189 to 257 men at the Alamo, a place where he swore he would fight until he died. No one is sure of the exact number of men who defended the Alamo, but the official list totals 189.[1]

Austin Recruits Troops

The Mexican government decided to send large battalions of men to the Texas region and stop any further problems. There were also orders in place to arrest Travis and others like him. Colonists in the town of Gonzales elected Austin to lead their makeshift volunteer army. His plan was to go to Bexar where most agreed that a pivotal battle against the Mexicans would take place.

▲ *William Travis decided to use the Alamo as a gathering point for his troops.*

But his army soon fell apart because the soldiers were not very disciplined. Disappointed, he decided to go to the United States and try and round up an American army to help. He would compare the plight of the Texans to that of American colonists' years earlier against the oppression of England.

Travis at the Alamo

Meanwhile, the Alamo became the gathering point for the volunteer troops that were left behind and included some soldiers who answered to William Travis, who was quickly becoming known for being a tough leader who kept his troops in line. Sam Houston, who was away from the garrison trying to talk the Cherokee out of aiding the Mexican Army, wrote letters to the men of the Alamo. He told them that perhaps they should retreat until they have a bigger force to face the impending attack from the oncoming Mexican Army. He did not think that San Antonio, where the Alamo was located, would play an important role in the battle for Texas independence.

General Santa Anna was leading a massive display of force north toward Texas. He planned to squash this rebellion once and for all in an unyielding show of might that would most certainly spell the end of the Texas movement for independence forever.

Many movies have been made about the events that occurred during Texas's fight for independence, including Walt Disney's *Davy Crockett at the Alamo*. View more images related to the thirteen-day siege of the Alamo at the **Alamo Images: Changing Perceptions of a Texas Experience** Web site.

▷ David "Davy" Crockett

It was during this time that an American legend, fresh from losing reelection to the United States Congress, headed south to Texas with a group of loyal followers. He had served two terms in Congress, killed 105 bears in one year, wrote his own life story, was the subject of theatrical plays, and became a living legend. His name was David "Davy" Crockett.

While historians agree that Crockett followed in the footsteps of Daniel Boone as the ultimate

American frontiersman hero, many of the tales associated with Crockett are exaggerations and were meant as tall tales. One outrageous story had him killing a bear when he was only three years old.

▷ Some Things However are Certain

Crockett was born in 1786 in Tennessee and by the time he was twelve years old, he had run away from home a few times. He supported himself as a waggoner, day laborer, and by doing odd jobs. Eventually he would return home and get an education.

In 1813, already married with two children, Crockett enlisted in the militia as a scout. On November 3, under the leadership of Andrew Jackson, Crockett participated in the massacre of the American Indian village of Tallusahatchee. This was done in retaliation for an American Indian attack on a white settlement.

Crockett was a successful military man and he continued moving up the ranks. On more than one occasion, he was charged with removing American Indians from certain areas where whites wanted to settle.

Crockett's first foray into the world of politics came when he took the job as justice of the peace. Soon after, he was convinced to run for town commissioner of Lawrenceberg. He was also elected colonel of the 57th militia regiment.

In 1821, Crockett ran successfully for a seat in the Tennessee Legislature. He later ran for congress and lost before running again and winning. But constant battles with President Andrew Jackson put an end to Crockett's political career when a Jackson supporter defeated Crockett during a reelection bid.

Crockett was known as an incredible hunter, sharpshooter, and great storyteller, often mixing fact and fiction to create a good yarn. Several stories and books, and even a Broadway play, were written about Crockett. But he set many of the stories and exaggerations straight when he wrote his autobiography, *A Narrative of the Life of David Crockett of the State of Tennessee.*

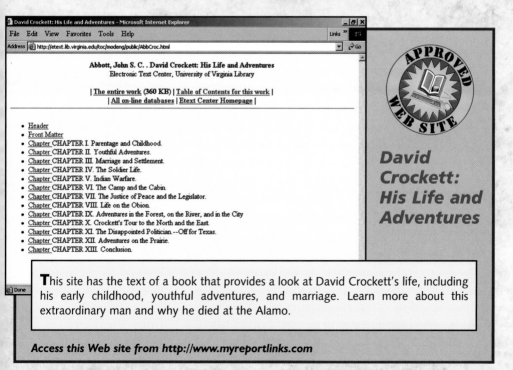

David Crockett: His Life and Adventures

This site has the text of a book that provides a look at David Crockett's life, including his early childhood, youthful adventures, and marriage. Learn more about this extraordinary man and why he died at the Alamo.

Access this Web site from http://www.myreportlinks.com

When he arrived in Texas, Crockett volunteered for a six-month enlistment in the Provisional Army of Texas. He was hoping to enter the world of Texas politics and be elected when he got out of the army. After arriving in Texas, Crockett spent a few weeks hunting and exploring the Texas countryside. Early in February he reported for active duty in Bexar.

Crockett Finds His Next Adventure

It is unclear to scholars whether Crockett went down to Texas simply to acquire vast lots of land as he told people, or that he went down there to try and wrestle power away from Sam Houston. After all, Houston was close friends with Andrew Jackson, Crockett's political enemy. Most people believe that Crockett and his group of rowdy travelers were merely looking for an adventure.[2] He soon found one in the Alamo.

Crockett learned that a battle would soon be taking place at the Alamo. He did not like the fact that the Mexicans were sending such a large army against a tiny group of ragtag soldiers. When he arrived at the Alamo, Crockett immediately lifted the spirits of the men who were stationed there waiting for Santa Anna's army to arrive. Many of the men had heard of the great David Crockett and could hardly believe their eyes when he actually showed up in the flesh. Crockett is often depicted wearing buckskin clothes and a raccoon or coonskin cap. His skill as an expert rifleman was known throughout the United States and Mexico. Even the Mexican Army knew who David Crockett was. He was immediately given the title of Commander of the Tennessee Mounted Volunteers. But he just wanted to be regarded as another private in the small army that he hoped would save Texas.

Jim Bowie

In addition to Travis and Crockett, there was another leader present at the Alamo with a group of soldiers already loyal to him. That man's name was James Bowie.

Bowie was born in Kentucky in 1796 but moved to Louisiana with his family when he was still a boy. It was there that he earned the reputation of being an adventurer. Some accounts say that Bowie would capture and ride wild horses. He also accumulated a lot of wealth by buying property and slaves. He and his brother bought slaves at bargain prices from famed pirate Jean Laffite. He would then resell the slaves at a higher price. Bowie was often credited with inventing a gigantic knife known as the Bowie knife but it was actually his brother who invented it.

During these years, Bowie made many enemies of people who did not approve of his business

▲ Jim Bowie was a famous adventurer, frontiersman, and soldier even before he joined the forces at the Alamo.

dealings. One such man, Morris Wright—a banker and a sheriff—tried shooting Bowie after they had an argument with one another. He missed, and after that encounter, Bowie's brother, Rezin, gave him an enormous butcher knife to start carrying around with him, according to *The Handbook of Texas History Online.*[3] He used it to kill two men who attacked him during a later duel and soon the gigantic knife became known as the Bowie knife. Men throughout the south and the west began asking blacksmiths to make them knives like Bowie's.

▷ Opportunity in Texas

Business became boring for Jim Bowie and so—like many others before him—he moved to Texas for a chance at adventure and cheap land. It was there that he met his future wife, Ursula. He served in the Mexican Army for her father in battles against the Comanche Indians. Bowie earned a reputation for being a fierce fighter who was not afraid to use that gigantic knife of his.

During his encounters with American Indians, Bowie tried making friends with some tribes and went to battle against others. Rumor had it that Bowie was solely interested in finding the near-mythical Los Almagres mines where riches of gold and silver were supposed to have been hidden. Some people said that Bowie was successful in

△ *Jim Bowie first went to Texas to buy cheap land. He soon married Ursula Veramendi, the daughter of an important Tejano landowner. This was the Palace of Veramendi, owned by the Veramendi family.*

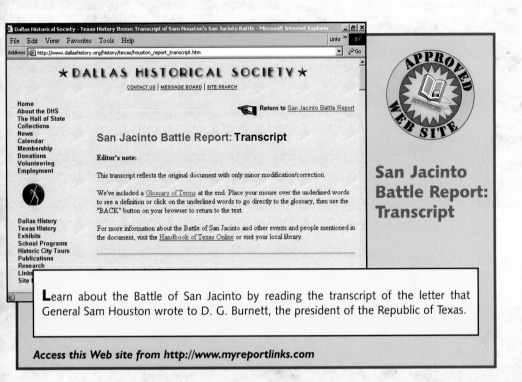

CONTACT US | MESSAGE BOARD | SITE SEARCH

Home
About the DHS
The Hall of State
Collections
News
Calendar
Membership
Donations
Volunteering
Employment

Dallas History
Texas History
Exhibits
School Programs
Historic City Tours
Publications
Research
Links
Site

☞ Return to San Jacinto Battle Report

San Jacinto Battle Report: Transcript

Editor's note:

This transcript reflects the original document with only minor modification/correction.

We've included a Glossary of Terms at the end. Place your mouse over the underlined words to see a definition or click on the underlined words to go directly to the glossary, then use the "BACK" button on your browser to return to the text.

For more information about the Battle of San Jacinto and other events and people mentioned in the document, visit the Handbook of Texas Online or visit your local library.

**San Jacinto
Battle Report:
Transcript**

Learn about the Battle of San Jacinto by reading the transcript of the letter that General Sam Houston wrote to D. G. Burnett, the president of the Republic of Texas.

Access this Web site from http://www.myreportlinks.com

finding the mines near San Saba and became a rich man.

But soon tragedy was to strike. While away on a short business trip Bowie's family became sick with cholera and died. Bowie was so distraught and heartbroken that he turned to drinking and soon became a drunk.

▷ Who's In Charge?

The Alamo was lucky to have three capable leaders in Crockett, Bowie, and Travis. But that also proved to be a curse, at least at first as volunteers and small amounts of soldiers appeared for duty. Because Travis was so young and because he really had not proven himself in battle, many of the older soldiers—especially Bowie's men—did not really respect him. They refused to follow his orders. If things did not get straightened out, there would be chaos at the Alamo. A vote was taken, and the men almost unanimously chose Bowie to lead the defense of the Alamo. But his drinking became worse and his thinking was not clear.

Travis threatened to leave the Alamo if the situation was not fixed. Finally an agreement was reached between Bowie and Travis: Bowie would be the leader of the volunteers and Travis would lead the regular army soldiers. They did not know it at the time, but their compromise could not have come at a better time.

General Santa Anna and his impressive army of at least sixty-five hundred men would be firing their cannon at the Alamo only nine days later.

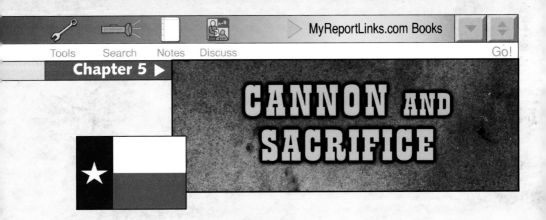

Chapter 5

CANNON AND SACRIFICE

Morale was low. Most of these men at the Alamo did not expect any real fighting to take place or at least any real threat of danger. It was almost as if the threat from Santa Anna was just a fantastic tale of phantoms. After all, why would Santa Anna bother with a handful of soldiers claiming an old Catholic mission as their own?

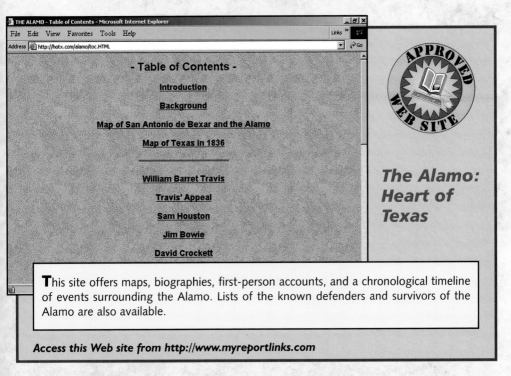

THE ALAMO - Table of Contents - Microsoft Internet Explorer

File   Edit   View   Favorites   Tools   Help   Links »

Address http://hotx.com/alamo/toc.HTML   Go

- Table of Contents -

Introduction

Background

Map of San Antonio de Bexar and the Alamo

Map of Texas in 1836

William Barret Travis

Travis' Appeal

Sam Houston

Jim Bowie

David Crockett

The Alamo: Heart of Texas

This site offers maps, biographies, first-person accounts, and a chronological timeline of events surrounding the Alamo. Lists of the known defenders and survivors of the Alamo are also available.

Access this Web site from http://www.myreportlinks.com

This romanticized account of the Battle of the Alamo was painted by Percy Moran.

▷ No Surrender!

Before they knew it, the "phantoms" appeared. That is when Colonel Travis decided to fire a cannon shot at the massing Mexican Army, letting them know that there would be no surrender. Then he decided to draw a line in the sand, giving those who did not want to fight a chance to leave the tiny mission that would surely become their grave. But the men were there to stay. They believed in freedom and were tired of the oppression the Mexican government had been dishing them.

Some think that Santa Anna had hoped to take Bexar, where the Alamo was located, by surprise. But his men encountered a little resistance in a nearby town called San Patricio. News of that attack that saw about twenty tejano soldiers killed or captured spread fast. The soldiers at the Alamo knew the Mexicans were coming and they were serious. Some also say that Santa Anna simply wanted to make an example of the "rebels" holed up inside the Alamo. He could have easily gone right past the Alamo and destroyed the Texas armed forces before they had a chance to fully form.

On the morning of February 23, 1836, the Mexican Army, led by Santa Anna, entered into San Antonio de Bexar. They did not quite know what to expect. After Travis sent his daring cannon shot toward the Mexicans, he and Bowie decided to craft a letter together asking the nearby town of Gonzales to send reinforcements. A few men responded to the letter and offered their services and fighting skills to the Alamo.

▷ Bombarded by Cannon

Santa Anna's full artillery had not yet arrived because huge cannon travel much slower than regular troops. But he decided to "soften" up the Alamo's defenses while keeping his men safe. He started daily firings of his cannon at the mission-turned-fortress. While Santa Anna shot his cannon, inflicting little damage, the men inside the Alamo shot their rifles and muskets and their long cannon and inflicted quite a number of casualties. As the days wore on there were little battles and skirmishes between the two parties.

It seemed as if the men from the Alamo were getting the better of the Mexican Army during these little skirmishes and cannon fire exchanges. After all, they were protected by the walls of the Alamo while the Mexican troops had little or no cover.

▷ Travis Asks for Help

This is about the time that Travis issued his famous appeal for help. The letter was printed many times and passed out among Texans and Americans. Without knowing it, Travis had stirred

This is a diorama that portrays the scene of the siege at the Alamo. This diorama was created from studies done by historians and the accounts of survivors.

a nation of people to the cause of the Alamo. People throughout the land knew that these brave men were surrounded. They also knew that if help did not arrive soon, all of them would wind up getting killed.

Travis received a letter back asking him to hold out for as long as possible. Help was said to be coming in the form of Colonel Fannin with three hundred men and four cannon. They would likely be there in three days time. But did Travis and the men of the Alamo have three more days? They had already held off the impressive Mexican force with cannon fire, sabotage, and bravery for a few days.

Travis also wrote a letter to David Ayers, the man who had custody of Travis's six-year-old son. He asked Ayers to relay the message that in the face of death, Travis knew that freedom was something worth dying for and he hoped that one day his son would be proud.

"Take care of my little boy," the letter states. "If the country should be spared then I may make him a great fortune. But if this country should be lost, and I should perish, he will have nothing but the proud recollection that he is the son of a man who died for his country."[1]

The Mexicans Move In

But by the morning of March 3, Santa Anna had grown impatient. He gathered his officers together

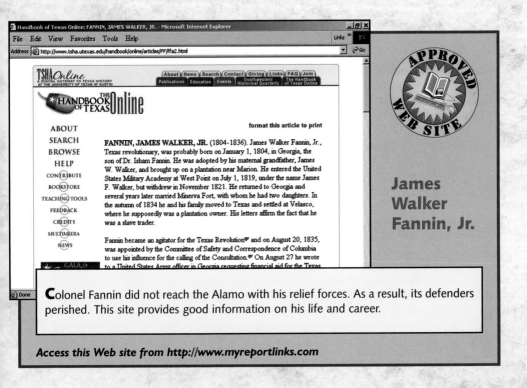

Handbook of Texas Online: FANNIN, JAMES WALKER, JR. - Microsoft Internet Explorer

File Edit View Favorites Tools Help

Address http://www.tsha.utexas.edu/handbook/online/articles/FF/ffa2.html

TSHAOnline
A DIGITAL GATEWAY TO TEXAS HISTORY
AT THE UNIVERSITY OF TEXAS AT AUSTIN

About News Search Contact Giving Links FAQ Join
Publications Education Events Southwestern Historical Quarterly The Handbook of Texas Online

HANDBOOK OF TEXAS Online

format this article to print

ABOUT
SEARCH
BROWSE
HELP
CONTRIBUTE
BOOKSTORE
TEACHING TOOLS
FEEDBACK
CREDITS
MULTIMEDIA
NEWS
GALA

FANNIN, JAMES WALKER, JR. (1804-1836). James Walker Fannin, Jr., Texas revolutionary, was probably born on January 1, 1804, in Georgia, the son of Dr. Isham Fannin. He was adopted by his maternal grandfather, James W. Walker, and brought up on a plantation near Marion. He entered the United States Military Academy at West Point on July 1, 1819, under the name James F. Walker, but withdrew in November 1821. He returned to Georgia and several years later married Minerva Fort, with whom he had two daughters. In the autumn of 1834 he and his family moved to Texas and settled at Velasco, where he supposedly was a plantation owner. His letters affirm the fact that he was a slave trader.

Fannin became an agitator for the Texas Revolution and on August 20, 1835, was appointed by the Committee of Safety and Correspondence of Columbia to use his influence for the calling of the Consultation. On August 27 he wrote to a United States Army officer in Georgia requesting financial aid for the Texas

James Walker Fannin, Jr.

Colonel Fannin did not reach the Alamo with his relief forces. As a result, its defenders perished. This site provides good information on his life and career.

Access this Web site from http://www.myreportlinks.com

and asked them if they thought he should attack now or wait four days for the bigger cannon to arrive. The larger cannon, his officers argued, would spare the lives of many Mexican soldiers. But Santa Anna said that there is glory in dying in battle. Plans were readied to attack the Alamo.

Remember that Santa Anna idolized the French general Napoléon. Napoléon believed it was a general's duty to sacrifice the blood of his soldiers to give glory to his nation. The long cannon were only a few days away from being delivered to Bexar. It is debatable whether there was any glory in losing men to the small gathering

"Dawn at the Alamo," a painting created by artist Henry McArdle in 1905.

defending the Alamo when they probably could have waited for the canon and won easily.

Colonel Fannin had already decided that it would be too dangerous to bring his three hundred men to aid Travis. He said that he was worried the cannon he was traveling with would fall into the wrong hands.

Santa Anna Rallies His Troops

In written orders given to his military leaders, Santa Anna reminded the men of their "duty" to their country:

> The honor of the nation being interested in this engagement against bold and lawless foreigners who are opposing us, His Excellency expects that every man will do his duty, and exert himself to give a day of glory to the country, and of the gratification of the Supreme Government, who will know how to reward the distinguished deeds of the brave soldiers of the Army of Operations.[2]

Shortly after midnight, March 6, 1836, the Mexican soldiers began creeping closer and closer to the fortified mission. Their plan was to get as close as possible to the fort and then mount an all-out surprise attack complete with rifles, cannon and men carrying ladders to get up over the fortified walls. There were sentinels, or soldiers keeping night watch, positioned in the Alamo. Either these men fell asleep or they just did

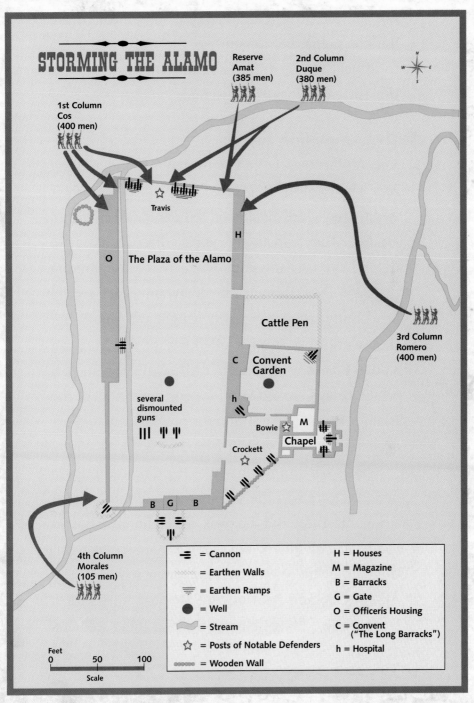

STORMING THE ALAMO

Reserve
Amat
(385 men)

2nd Column
Duque
(380 men)

1st Column
Cos
(400 men)

Travis

H

O

The Plaza of the Alamo

Cattle Pen

Convent
Garden

3rd Column
Romero
(400 men)

C

h

several
dismounted
guns

Bowie

M

Chapel

Crockett

B G B

4th Column
Morales
(105 men)

= Cannon

= Earthen Walls

= Earthen Ramps

= Well

= Stream

= Posts of Notable Defenders

= Wooden Wall

H = Houses

M = Magazine

B = Barracks

G = Gate

O = Officer's Housing

C = Convent
   ("The Long Barracks")

h = Hospital

Feet
0   50   100

Scale

△ *This map shows the strategy of Santa Anna's army as they laid siege on the men at The Alamo.*

not see the advancing enemy troops through the darkness. Just before sunrise, the word was given to attack. Santa Anna used 1,400 men to attack the 180 or so inside the Alamo.

Overwhelming Attack

The Alamo was pelted with cannon and musket fire. The men of the Alamo were startled in their sleep. They were awakened to hear battle cries and gunfire. They ran to the walls, rifles in hand, to defend the tiny mission. There was panic among the men. Even though they knew an attack would be coming, they were still caught off guard. Yet they were able to pick off many of the Mexican soldiers as they approached the wall. For a short while, things looked good for the defenders of the Alamo. But soon the number of Mexican soldiers attacking the fort was just too much.

Travis tried to inspire his sleepy, scared men to action. He ran to the top of the wall and started firing his rifle. But he was immediately shot in the head and killed. With Bowie too sick to fight, the men of the Alamo were without a leader. The Alamo's cannon held off the Mexican surge for a short while, killing many of the oncoming soldiers.

The Tide Turns

No one knows for sure what happened next or how long the battle lasted. But most historians

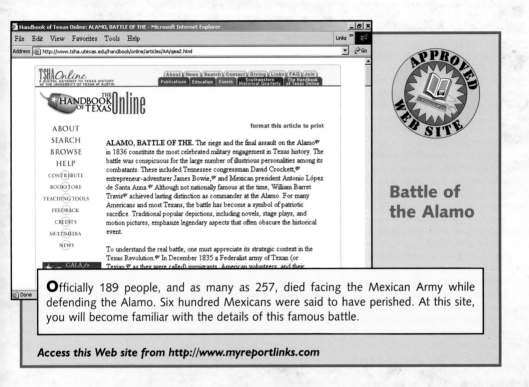

**Battle of
the Alamo**

Officially 189 people, and as many as 257, died facing the Mexican Army while defending the Alamo. Six hundred Mexicans were said to have perished. At this site, you will become familiar with the details of this famous battle.

Access this Web site from http://www.myreportlinks.com

and experts agree that the men of the Alamo held their positions and fought fiercely for as long as they could. The battle lasted between one and five hours and there was often hand-to-hand fighting going on. Eventually the men of the Alamo retreated into positions in the small buildings inside the Alamo. While this gave them cover, it also meant that the battle was essentially over. The Mexicans were able to take the cannon of the Alamo and turn them on the very buildings that housed the volunteer soldiers.

The Mexicans eventually went from room to room looking for soldiers to kill. Remember, the attack was under the premise that no quarter be given. That meant that none of the fighters inside the Alamo would be taken prisoner. They would all be killed.

▷ Deaths of Bowie and Crockett

By this time, Jim Bowie, who was confined to his room, could not participate in the fight because he was too sick. Historians say that he had loaded pistols at the ready and fired upon the Mexicans when they entered his room. He was already dying but wanted to control when and how he died. Like Travis, Bowie was killed.

The exact nature of David Crockett's fate at the Alamo is not known for certain except that the former adventurer and congressman died. Some reports say that he was one of the last soldiers found by the Mexicans. Mexican accounts of the battle say that he tried to surrender and was then killed. Other accounts say he was captured and taken before Santa Anna where he was executed by soldiers who ran him through with their swords. Other reports say that he was simply killed in battle.

But historian James A. Shackford said it is not very important how Davy Crockett died. But instead how he lived. Shackford also said that the most important thing to note was that Crockett fought and died at the Alamo along with everyone else. Being there and dying there was enough to make him a hero.[3]

▷ The Spirit of the Texans

Whether it was one hour of five hours long, the Battle of the Alamo did little from a military standpoint. While some of the estimated Mexican deaths are put at six hundred, the number of Mexican soldiers killed has been disputed. No, the real damage done to the Mexican Army was a psychological one. The Battle at the Alamo showed the Mexicans that these volunteers, these Texans, were willing to die for their freedom. The power of being faced with that notion can not be measured.

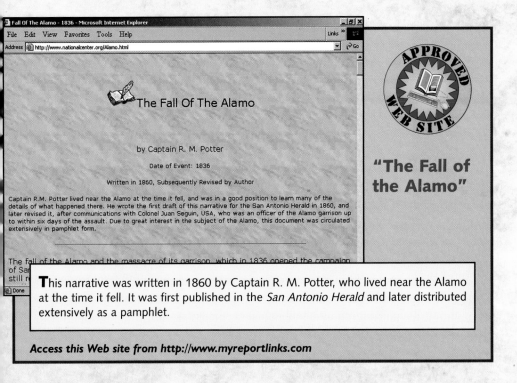

"The Fall of the Alamo"

This narrative was written in 1860 by Captain R. M. Potter, who lived near the Alamo at the time it fell. It was first published in the *San Antonio Herald* and later distributed extensively as a pamphlet.

Access this Web site from http://www.myreportlinks.com

The fact that the soldiers inside the Alamo delayed Santa Anna's attack for nearly two weeks, also bought time for the Texans to put together a ragtag army that would face Santa Anna later on. Santa Anna might have been better off if he had just attacked the Alamo when his men first arrived on the scene in February.

▷ **Survivors**

One of the Alamo's survivors was Susannah Dickinson. Along with her young daughter, she refused to leave the Alamo—choosing instead to

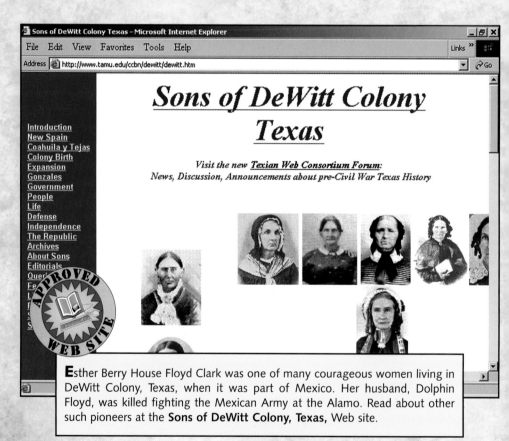

Sons of DeWitt Colony Texas - Microsoft Internet Explorer

File Edit View Favorites Tools Help

Address http://www.tamu.edu/ccbn/dewitt/dewitt.htm

Sons of DeWitt Colony Texas

Introduction
New Spain
Coahuila y Tejas
Colony Birth
Expansion
Gonzales
Government
People
Life
Defense
Independence
The Republic
Archives
About Sons
Editorials

Visit the new *Texian Web Consortium Forum*:
News, Discussion, Announcements about pre-Civil War Texas History

Esther Berry House Floyd Clark was one of many courageous women living in DeWitt Colony, Texas, when it was part of Mexico. Her husband, Dolphin Floyd, was killed fighting the Mexican Army at the Alamo. Read about other such pioneers at the **Sons of DeWitt Colony, Texas,** Web site.

stay in the old mission to support her husband, Almeron Dickinson, and his compatriots in their battle for Texas independence.

Her husband was killed, and Susannah herself received a bullet wound to her leg. Luckily, her baby was unharmed, and they were soon let go after being captured by some of Santa Anna's men. One of the Mexican officers reportedly offered to marry her and take care of her little baby but Susannah refused.

Later she would become a valuable source as one of the only eyewitnesses to the heroics and Battle of the Alamo. Her accounts of what happened there in 1836 have been questioned because when she was pressed she was known to do or say anything for money.

▷ Guerrero and Joe

Some of the other survivors included Mexican deserter Brigido Guerrero and Travis's slave named Joe.

Guerrero had left the Mexican Army to fight alongside those seeking independence from oppression. As the fall of the Alamo became imminent, he stopped fighting and acted as if he had been a prisoner of the Texans. When the Mexicans overtook the fort, he did some quick talking and made up a story of being captured. This saved his life. After the revolution, Guerrero settled in San Antonio, Texas, with his wife.

Joe was long Travis's personal slave. Testifying before inquiries shortly after the battle took place, Joe claimed that he followed Travis into battle and fired his weapon at the oncoming Mexican soldiers. He then retreated into one of the buildings and fired his weapon from there. Finally, when the fort was overrun, Joe was reportedly shot by a pistol and stabbed with a bayonet point. But he lived and was captured by the Mexicans before being released.

After giving his account of the battle, Joe was sent back to the Travis estate where he was to remain a slave. Even after all that, he was not granted his freedom. But one year later, he managed to escape. He was never captured or heard from again.[4]

▷ Changing the Tide

The fact that Santa Anna sacrificed men and did not wait for the large cannon also had some of his officers questioning his military skills. The soldiers were not as confident as they were before the Battle of the Alamo. Was the glory worth it? They started hearing rumors of Sam Houston building a formidable army of Americans that would be ready for them.

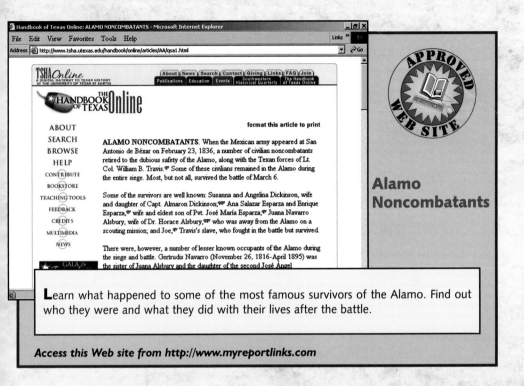

Alamo Noncombatants

Learn what happened to some of the most famous survivors of the Alamo. Find out who they were and what they did with their lives after the battle.

Access this Web site from http://www.myreportlinks.com

One hour or five, word spread quickly through Texas about the incredible bravery and sacrifice of the men of the Alamo. The slaughter made supporters of Texan independence angry and inspired them. It made people realize that the time had come to take a stand. The courage showed at the Alamo galvanized Texas. Their heroic struggle would never be forgotten.

Soon the battle cry was "Remember the Alamo."

Chapter 6

TEXAS INDEPENDENCE AND STATEHOOD

The Alamo was lost. And now, those who sought Texas independence looked to Sam Houston and Colonel Fannin as their last hopes. Soon, Santa Anna would track down Houston's army for a final

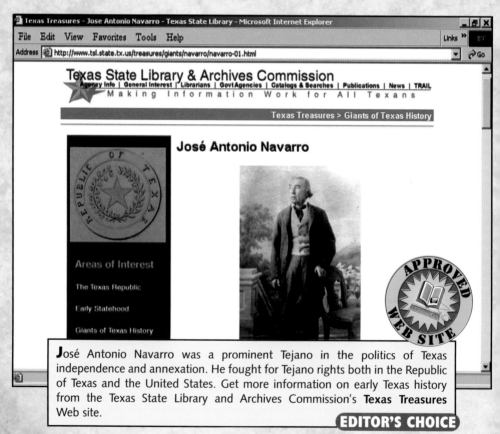

José Antonio Navarro was a prominent Tejano in the politics of Texas independence and annexation. He fought for Tejano rights both in the Republic of Texas and the United States. Get more information on early Texas history from the Texas State Library and Archives Commission's **Texas Treasures** Web site.

EDITOR'S CHOICE

showdown. No one gave the Texans much of a chance.

Houston's Army

Sam Houston was officially named the commander-in-chief of the Texas armed forces on March 7, 1836, before he left Washington-on-the-Brazos. On March 11, five days after the Alamo fell, Houston reached the town of Gonzales and found a group of 374 men who just received news about the Alamo.

They were angry and wanted to fight. Now, Houston's army was shaping up. He sent word to Fannin to send his men along, too. With both their small armies, they could provide Santa Anna with a formidable opponent. But once again Fannin did not respond quickly.

With Santa Anna's army bearing down, Houston decided his best course of action—until Fannin arrived with help—was to burn down the town and retreat. Back then, retreating armies often burned down a town it was leaving so that the approaching army would not be able to stay there.

Fannin's Troops

One week later, Fannin's forces were involved in a battle in the town of Coleto. Fannin's men took heavy losses so he evacuated the town. But it was too late. His forces were surrounded by a column

Sam Houston was at a meeting in Washington-on-the-Brazos when the Alamo fell to the Mexicans. He responded by rallying the remaining Texas soldiers.

of Mexican soldiers. Fannin either was lied to or he did not know that the Mexican Army was not taking prisoners. His men, nearly four hundred strong, were taken back to Goliad. They were shot and killed by the Mexican Army. Fannin himself had been wounded in the previous fighting. He was executed as well.

The war was nearly over. It seemed the Texas Army had been destroyed. Santa Anna would try to drive the remaining forces from Mexican territory, probably into Louisiana.

Santa Anna could smell blood. He knew that if he defeated the Texans that his name could go right next to his idol, Napoléon, in the history books. It was not to be.

▷ Santa Anna's Mistake

What happened next was a stroke of luck for the Texans seeking independence. Santa Anna had learned that rebel leaders were holed up in nearby Harrisburg. Instead of sending his army there, Santa Anna himself took only five hundred of his men on a mission to capture, then kill, the rebel leaders. It would turn out to be a careless and overconfident mistake that would likely cost Mexico the war and Santa Anna any chance at greatness.

By the time Santa Anna arrived in Harrisburg the rebel leaders, or Texas government,

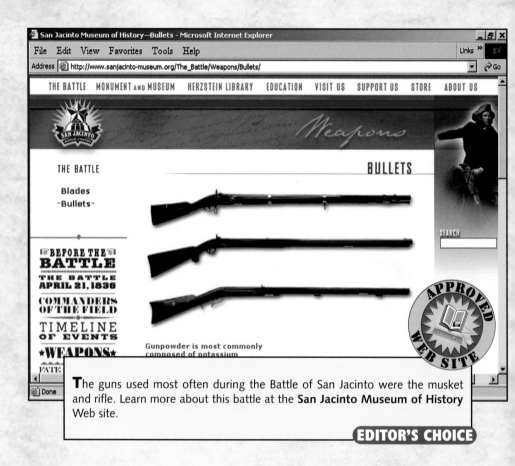

San Jacinto Museum of History—Bullets - Microsoft Internet Explorer

File   Edit   View   Favorites   Tools   Help   Links »

Address http://www.sanjacinto-museum.org/The_Battle/Weapons/Bullets/   Go

THE BATTLE   MONUMENT AND MUSEUM   HERZSTEIN LIBRARY   EDUCATION   VISIT US   SUPPORT US   STORE   ABOUT US

Weapons

THE BATTLE   BULLETS

Blades
-Bullets-

SEARCH

⟪BEFORE THE⟫
BATTLE
THE BATTLE
APRIL 21, 1836

COMMANDERS
OF THE FIELD

TIMELINE
OF EVENTS

★WEAPONS★

FATE

Gunpowder is most commonly
composed of potassium

The guns used most often during the Battle of San Jacinto were the musket and rifle. Learn more about this battle at the **San Jacinto Museum of History** Web site.

APPROVED WEB SITE

EDITOR'S CHOICE

had already escaped. He burned the town down. But now he was cut off from the bulk of his army, although he still had the five hundred soldiers at his command. This was finally Sam Houston's chance to get to Santa Anna without having to defeat his entire army. But Santa Anna was not worried. He was confident that he would be able to catch Houston's ragtag army and defeat them once and for all. He had become a little too confident.

▷ Texan Offensive

Suddenly, Houston went on the offensive, or at least became a player in this cat-and-mouse game. He went into Harrisburg after Santa Anna. A few days later Santa Anna and his men arrived at a place known as Morgan's Point while Houston was crossing an area known as Buffalo Bayou. The names are not as important as where the two military leaders were heading. They were both being drawn toward the San Jacinto River—where the battle for Texas independence would be decided at last.

▷ Battle of San Jacinto

On the morning of April 20, the two forces were only about a mile apart. Houston's men urged him to attack but he wanted to wait. His men became frustrated, so he allowed them to take potshots and little attacks on Santa Anna's men. He did not want a full-scale attack. Here, he nearly made the mistake that Fannin did. By not acting when he had the opportunity, Houston allowed Santa Anna to send for reinforcements. The following morning, much to Houston's chagrin, another 650 Mexican troops arrived to assist their general. Now the sides were about even, with Houston and Santa Anna boasting about twelve hundred men apiece. The time for talking, negotiating, and running was over.

The first thing Houston did was to send men to destroy a bridge near Buffalo Bayou so that the Mexican Army would not be able to retreat. What happened next was astounding. Even though the Texan Army was only a mile away and within sight on many occasions, the Mexican Army was caught unprepared. They were resting and feeding their horses as well as eating. Santa Anna himself had posted no sentries, sentinels, or scouts and was taking a nap when Houston's men attacked. They screamed "Remember the Alamo!" over and over again as they overwhelmed the Mexicans with sheer determination and revenge. The surprise attack took place in broad daylight and was a great military strategy for Houston.

"The deaths of the Bexar Garrison and others lost at the Alamo had been avenged," wrote historian Richard Bruce Winders.[1]

▷ Mexican Retreat

Houston's men could not be restrained. They chased many of the fleeing Mexicans who were screaming that they were not responsible for the Alamo into the swamps and boggy marshes where they were slaughtered. Even their horses were killed.[2]

The main battle itself lasted less than a half hour according to historic documents, but the fighting continued for about four hours. When the

▲ Sam Houston and his troops crossed the Buffalo Bayou on their way to the Battle of San Jacinto. This photo shows what Buffalo Bayou looked like in 1968.

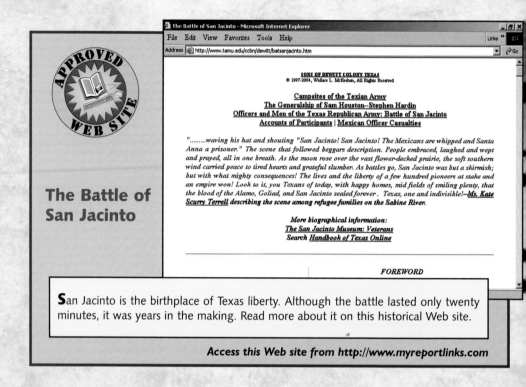

The Battle of San Jacinto

Campsites of the Texian Army
The Generalship of Sam Houston--Stephen Hardin
Officers and Men of the Texas Republican Army: Battle of San Jacinto
Accounts of Participants | Mexican Officer Casualties

"........waving his hat and shouting "San Jacinto! San Jacinto! The Mexicans are whipped and Santa Anna a prisoner." The scene that followed beggars description. People embraced, laughed and wept and prayed, all in one breath. As the moon rose over the vast flower-decked prairie, the soft southern wind carried peace to tired hearts and grateful slumber. As battles go, San Jacinto was but a skirmish; but with what mighty consequences! The lives and the liberty of a few hundred pioneers at stake and an empire won! Look to it, you Texans of today, with happy homes, mid fields of smiling plenty, that the blood of the Alamo, Goliad, and San Jacinto sealed forever. Texas, one and indivisible!--Ms. Kate Scurry Terrell describing the scene among refugee families on the Sabine River.

More biographical information:
The San Jacinto Museum: Veterans
Search *Handbook of Texas Online*

FOREWORD

San Jacinto is the birthplace of Texas liberty. Although the battle lasted only twenty minutes, it was years in the making. Read more about it on this historical Web site.

Access this Web site from http://www.myreportlinks.com

fighting stopped, it was akin to a massacre. The Texans only lost nine men while they killed 630 Mexican soldiers and captured about 730. But Santa Anna himself was among the missing.

▷ **Somehow he had Escaped. Or had he?**
The next morning, April 22, 1836, Houston sent scouts out near the river. They came back with General Santa Anna himself! He was caught hiding along the banks of the river.

Houston's men begged their new leader to execute Santa Anna just as he had executed so many Texans—even those who had surrendered under

Fannin's command. It was only fair, they argued, that Santa Anna should suffer the same fate.

But what Houston decided was infinitely smarter. He knew how important Santa Anna could be to the Texas push for independence if he were kept alive. The Texas government had its first hostage and he was an extremely important one.

▷ Treaty of Velasco

A peace agreement was negotiated. Santa Anna hoped the agreement would simply save his life. He also never dreamed that his loss and capture would be seen by the Mexican people as a tremendous failure. He believed that he would be able to retain power and continue to lead the young nation.

On May 14, Santa Anna agreed at gunpoint to sign what would become known as the Treaty of Velasco. It would end the war between the parties and recognize Texas as an independent country. Texas would no longer be under the grip of the Mexican government or military. The Mexican government was very angry at Santa Anna for this, and for many years did not respect the peace agreement that was made.

But that was not the end for the leader who patterned himself after Napoléon. He would go on to become the dominant figure in Mexican politics for decades to come. However, after his loss to Houston at San Jacinto, the Mexican government

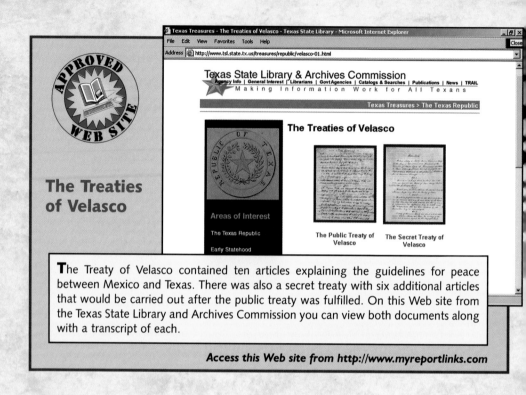

The Treaties of Velasco

Texas State Library & Archives Commission
Agency Info | General Interest | Librarians | Govt Agencies | Catalogs & Searches | Publications | News | TRAIL
Making Information Work for All Texans

Texas Treasures > The Texas Republic

The Treaties of Velasco

Areas of Interest

The Texas Republic

Early Statehood

The Public Treaty of Velasco

The Secret Treaty of Velasco

The Treaty of Velasco contained ten articles explaining the guidelines for peace between Mexico and Texas. There was also a secret treaty with six additional articles that would be carried out after the public treaty was fulfilled. On this Web site from the Texas State Library and Archives Commission you can view both documents along with a transcript of each.

Access this Web site from http://www.myreportlinks.com

was thrown into chaos that some say they never have recovered from.

However, right after the treaties were signed, Santa Anna traveled to Washington where he met with President Andrew Jackson. He then retired to private life and stayed out of politics for a couple of years. His retirement would not last long.

▷ Return of Santa Anna

Between the years of 1833 and 1855, Mexico had thirty-six different presidents, including Santa Anna himself eleven times! It seemed that no matter how miserably Santa Anna failed or how many enemies he made, he was still able to seize power when he wanted. For example, only three years after the crushing loss at San Jacinto, Santa Anna became popular among the Mexican people again when he defeated invading French forces at Vera Cruz in 1838.

The French, sensing that Mexico was weak, decided to invade in an effort to expand their colonial holdings. But Santa Anna proved that he could not only be a good military leader, but he was a fierce warrior as well. During the battle at Vera Cruz, several of the horses he was riding were shot out from under him, and he even lost half a leg in battle. But he continued fighting until the battle was won and the French were repressed.

In an odd occurrence that shows how attention-hungry Santa Anna really was, he had the half a leg dug up four years later in 1842 and placed it in a monument for people to see. People forgot his military blunders that cost Mexico the area of Texas and forgave him. He used the leg to prove that no one was more committed to Mexico than he was. It worked. He formed new political allies and became president again.

Santa Anna as a Leader of the People

While Santa Anna was a tough leader with his enemies, he was never ruthless with his power. He would force his enemies into exile rather than have them killed as some leaders did and still do.

▲ This political cartoon shows the artist's impression of Santa Anna and Mexican general Martin Perfecto de Cos's surrender to Sam Houston. This cartoon reflects the anti-Mexican feelings in the United States at the time.

Historians say that Santa Anna loved being in control but did not like the responsibilities of having to run the country. He often left that work for others to do, and they did not do it well. By 1844 the country had grown tired of years of broken promises. In a crushing blow to his ego, Santa Anna was once again removed from power. He was exiled.

But a few years later, in 1846, he returned and was given an army to fight the Mexican-American War against the Americans who were advancing into Mexico to take more land. It was another terrible loss for the Mexicans.

Fade From Power

Incredibly, he returned to power but did something that caused the Mexican people to revolt and send him back into exile. Because the country needed money, he sold millions of acres of land in what are now Arizona and New Mexico to the United States. This was known as the Gadsden Purchase. He was deposed, jailed, and sent back to exile. He returned a few more times to occupy the leadership of the country but never again regained the glory he once had.

The end for Santa Anna was a sad one. He lost all of his money and his power. He loved to tell battle stories, so his wife would pay journalists to come and interview him—something that Santa Anna never knew about. He died in 1876.

President Houston

Based mainly on his heroic deeds in battle and his victory over Santa Anna, Houston was elected president of Texas. Stephen Austin, though, had returned from the United States—where he was trying to find financial backers for the war for

Texas Treasures - Sam Houston - Texas State Library - Microsoft Internet Explorer

File   Edit   View   Favorites   Tools   Help   Links »

Address | http://www.tsl.state.tx.us/treasures/giants/houston-01.html   Go

He entered Texas in December 1832 and was immediately swept into the ferment of political activity. He was a delegate to the Convention of 1833, the Consultation, and the Convention of 1836. He was appointed major general in the regular army by the Consultation and was made commander in chief by the Convention of 1836. Also during this period, he negotiated a treaty with the Cherokee on February 3, 1836.

President Houston's Official Residence, 1837

The battle of San Jacinto brought the active war to a close on April 21, 1836. The capture of president/general Santa Anna the next day gave Houston the upper hand in negotiating with the Mexican troops remaining in the country. A few days later, he was taken to the United

Sam Houston lived in this shack during his time as president of the Republic of Texas. Get more information on early Texas history from the Texas State Library and Archives Commission's **Texas Treasures** Web site.

EDITOR'S CHOICE

independence. Austin wanted to be president very badly and made his intentions known. But he lost by a whopping five thousand votes to Houston. Austin became his secretary of state but died a few months later in December 1836. Houston served another term a few years after as well.

▷ Joining the United States

Soon after Houston's second term, on February 19, 1846, Texas was annexed into the United States and became a state. The move to become a state was a popular one among most Texans. The Texas government had negotiated for several years with the United States about becoming a state. Houston had wanted to get it done while he was president and some Texans viewed it as a failure that he was unable to accomplish it.

The United States had long wanted Texas to become part of their country. In fact, in 1826, President John Quincy Adams offered Mexico one million dollars for it. Four years later, President Andrew Jackson offered five million dollars for it. Finally, with the defeat of Santa Anna, it now became a possibility.

▷ The Path to Statehood

There were obstacles to statehood. First off, many American northerners did not want another southern state to join the union. The south and Texas were pro-slavery and another slave state just might throw the balance off. Secondly, many Texans spoke only Spanish and so there was a question as to how to deal with a bilingual state. Also, the American government was not sure how to deal with a state that was so large. Texas was four times larger than the already largest state. And remember, many of the people in Texas had gone there from the United States because they did not want too much government in their lives.

Even though the Mexican government had been opposed to slavery, they allowed American settlers to bring their slaves into Mexico and the area known as Texas. There were five thousand slaves in Texas by the time the Battle of the Alamo took place. Once Texas gained its independence, more and more slaves were bought and brought into Texas. By 1846 there were thirty thousand slaves in Texas. A slave to work in the fields would cost an owner eight hundred dollars to buy and a metal worker would cost about two thousand dollars. Slaves were very expensive and seen as a symbol of extreme wealth.

Slavery and Statehood

Most Americans and Texans wanted Texas to join the United States. But it would cause some political problems. Texas would be a slave state, and slave states would have more votes in Congress. The free states did not want this to happen, because then the slave states could pass laws favorable to the southern economy at the expense of the economy of the northern states.

From 1836 to 1845 the leaders of the Republic of Texas and the leaders of the United States could not agree on a treaty of annexation that would allow Texas to become part of the United States.

At one point, a frustrated American Congress passed a joint resolution that would allow Texas to join the union and break into four smaller states if it so desired. But Texas would not have the power

▲ President John Quincy Adams had tried to buy Texas from Mexico in 1826.

to secede from the union—a sticking point among some of the Texans.

Another problem was that in 1842, the Mexican government twice attacked Bexar to try and reclaim the land that Santa Anna had lost. While the Texans were able to fend off the attacks, there was worry that Great Britain—still angry at the United States for the Revolutionary War—would help the Mexicans defeat the Texans by offering military and financial aid.

In July 1845, the Texas Constitutional Convention met to discuss the annexation as well as another tricky matter: Mexico had offered Texas a treaty to end hostilities between Mexico and Texas

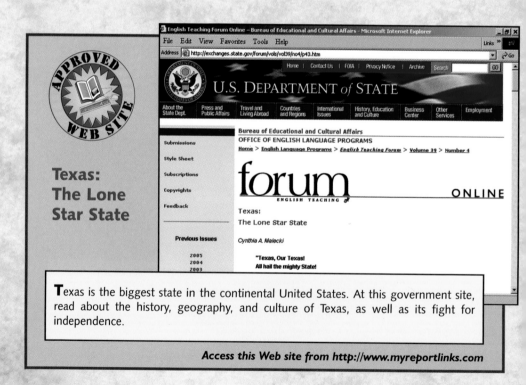

Texas:
The Lone
Star State

Texas is the biggest state in the continental United States. At this government site, read about the history, geography, and culture of Texas, as well as its fight for independence.

Access this Web site from http://www.myreportlinks.com

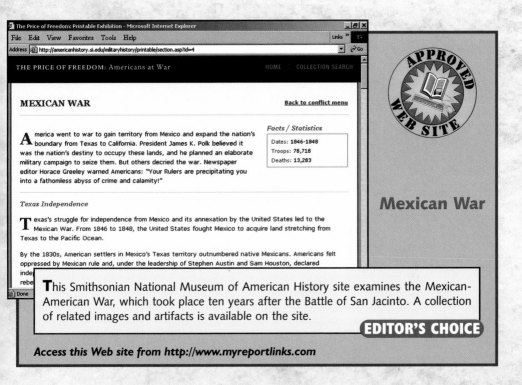

Mexican War

The Price of Freedom: Printable Exhibition - Microsoft Internet Explorer

File Edit View Favorites Tools Help   Links »

Address http://americanhistory.si.edu/militaryhistory/printable/section.asp?id=4   Go

THE PRICE OF FREEDOM: Americans at War   HOME   COLLECTION SEARCH

MEXICAN WAR   Back to conflict menu

America went to war to gain territory from Mexico and expand the nation's boundary from Texas to California. President James K. Polk believed it was the nation's destiny to occupy these lands, and he planned an elaborate military campaign to seize them. But others decried the war. Newspaper editor Horace Greeley warned Americans: "Your Rulers are precipitating you into a fathomless abyss of crime and calamity!"

Facts / Statistics

Dates: **1846-1848**
Troops: **78,718**
Deaths: **13,283**

Texas Independence

Texas's struggle for independence from Mexico and its annexation by the United States led to the Mexican War. From 1846 to 1848, the United States fought Mexico to acquire land stretching from Texas to the Pacific Ocean.

By the 1830s, American settlers in Mexico's Texas territory outnumbered native Mexicans. Americans felt oppressed by Mexican rule and, under the leadership of Stephen Austin and Sam Houston, declared inde
rebe

This Smithsonian National Museum of American History site examines the Mexican-American War, which took place ten years after the Battle of San Jacinto. A collection of related images and artifacts is available on the site.

EDITOR'S CHOICE

Access this Web site from http://www.myreportlinks.com

but only if Texas refused to join the United States. The Mexicans and Texans were fighting over lands that would eventually become New Mexico and southern Arizona. After much debate, the Texans agreed to be annexed. It was then ratified by Congress, and on December 29, 1845, Texas became a state of the union.

▷ The Civil War

When the Civil War started in the United States, Texas was square in the middle of the conflict—though not militarily. The Southern states pressured Texas to leave, or secede, from the nation in the war over whether to abolish slavery. The number

San Antonio, the site of the Battle of the Alamo, as it appears in modern times.

This political cartoon celebrates the annexation of Texas into the United States. The men holding the rope are the Whigs who were against annexation.

of slaves in Texas compared to free men and women was mind-boggling. By 1860, the census found 182,566 slaves living in the state. This represented over 30 percent of the total population of the state. Slaveowners were, by far, the wealthiest people in the state and the most active when it came to politics.

The slaves in Texas did not revolt or try to run away after news of the Civil War started to trickle down to them. They kept working and knew that a Union victory would result in their freedom. Texas was never invaded but on June 19, 1865, Union soldiers occupied Texas and freed all the slaves. That day is still celebrated in the African-American community and is known as Juneteenth.

▷ Sam Houston Bows Out

Sam Houston did not shy away from politics after his presidency was up. He became governor of the state and also served as a U.S. senator. He returned for one more turn as governor but was thrown from office when he refused to endorse the South's secession from the United States in 1861. He was a staunch believer in the United States republic, and it broke his heart when he was ousted and the state seceded. Even though he was against slavery, Houston tried to make both sides of the Texas debate compromise but was unsuccessful.

He did not want to see all the hard work and sacrifice—like those who died at the Alamo—be thrown away because rich Texans wanted to keep their slaves—something that he felt was cruel and evil.

Unfortunately, Sam Houston never lived to see the end of the Civil War and peace in his adopted land of Texas. He died of pneumonia on July 26, 1863, in Huntsville, Texas.

Report Links

The Internet sites described below can be accessed at http://www.myreportlinks.com

▶**The Alamo**
Editor's Choice Everything you ever wanted to know about the Alamo can be found on this site.

▶**Remember the Alamo**
Editor's Choice PBS brings us a series called *The Alamo*.

▶**Alamo Images: Changing Perceptions of a Texas Experience**
Editor's Choice See some of the earliest paintings and maps of the Alamo battle.

▶**Texas Treasures**
Editor's Choice Taking a look at Texas from the beginning.

▶**Mexican War**
Editor's Choice Read about the Mexican-American War on this Web site.

▶**San Jacinto Museum of History**
Editor's Choice Learn about the battle that ended Mexican rule over Texas.

▶*The Alamo: Heart of Texas*
This e-book offers in-depth information on the Alamo.

▶**Alamo Noncombatants**
A few survivors of the Alamo battle lived to tell the tale.

▶**The Alamo: 13 Days of Glory**
Take a closer look at the myths and mysteries surrounding the Alamo.

▶**Antonio López de Santa Anna**
Read a biography of General Antonio López de Santa Anna.

▶**The Avalon Project at Yale Law School: Texas—From Independence to Annexation**
Read historical documents related to the fight for Texas independence.

▶**Battle of the Alamo**
What really happened at the Alamo?

▶**Battle of the Alamo: Virtual Field Trip Network**
This is a good overview of the Alamo.

▶**The Battle of San Jacinto**
Written by a noted historian, this overview provides an interesting look at the battle.

▶**Daughters of the Republic of Texas Library**
The DRT library was founded to preserve the legacy of the Republic of Texas.

Report Links

The Internet sites described below can be accessed at http://www.myreportlinks.com

▶ **David Crockett: His Life and Adventures**

Read an electronic version of a book about David Crockett.

▶ **"The Fall of the Alamo"**

Read Captain R. M. Potter's account of the Alamo.

▶ **Hidalgo y Castilla, Miguel**

Father Hidalgo led a revolution in Mexico.

▶ **James Walker Fannin, Jr.**

Read a biography on James Walker Fannin.

▶ **Mexican Independence**

Learn about Mexico's defection from Spain.

▶ **Sam Houston**

An extensive look at the life of Sam Houston.

▶ **Sam Houston Memorial Museum**

This is a museum dedicated to the life of Sam Houston.

▶ **San Antonio De Valero Mission**

A Franciscan mission was the site for the Alamo.

▶ **San Jacinto Battle Report: Transcript**

This is a transcript of Sam Houston's account of the Battle of San Jacinto.

▶ **Sons of DeWitt Colony, Texas**

This organization is dedicated to the study of the DeWitt Colony from 1700–1846.

▶ **Stephen Fuller Austin**

This Texas State Historical Association Web site provides a biography of Austin.

▶ **Texas History**

This Web site is presented by the Dallas Historical Society.

▶ **Texas: The Lone Star State**

A short history of Texas is presented on this site.

▶ **The Treaties of Velasco**

The Texas State Library and Archives Commission has a copy of the Treaty of Velasco.

▶ **William Barret Travis**

This is an extensive look at the life of William Barret Travis.

allegiance—Loyalty to one's country.

annexation—To add a body of land to an existing country or state.

artillery—Weapons that attack through the air such as cannon, bow and arrows, catapults, and missiles.

brash—Overconfident or rash, without a concern for the bad things that may happen.

cannonade—An attack of heavy artillery fire.

cholera—An infectious intestinal disease caused by ingesting contaminated food or water.

coonskin cap—A hat made from the pelt of a raccoon, made famous by David Crockett.

Creole—A person of entirely Spanish blood born in Spanish America.

debtors' prison—A prison for people that were unable to pay the money they owed to creditors.

empresario—A person who was given a parcel of land from the Mexican or Spanish government in return for promoting settlement in that area.

encampment—A place where a group of people or soldiers has set up camp.

extradition—The surrender of an accused or convicted person from one authority to another.

garrison—A permanent military post.

hominy—Dried yellow or white field corn kernels that are hulled and degermed.

immune—Protected from catching or feeling the effects of a disease.

insurgency—An organized revolt to overthrow a government.

massacre—The deliberate killing of a large number of innocent people.

militia—A group of citizens who have formed a fighting force.

mission—A local church from which missionaries do religious work; often depends upon a larger religious organization for financial support.

New World—The Americas, as named by the Europeans.

Panic of 1819—Time of economic downturn in the United States when banks failed and many people lost money. Many feel this was caused by the policies of the Second Bank of the United States.

Texian—Anglo-American citizens of Texas at the time that Mexico controlled the area.

Tejano—A person of Mexican descent living in Texas.

tyranny—A government in which one ruler holds absolute power.

Chapter 1. The Alamo

1. Mike Cox, "Davy's Widow," *Texas Tales,* March 8, 2005, <http://www.texasescapes .com/MikeCoxTexasTales/228-Davy-Crocketts-Widow -Elizabeth-Patton-Crockett.htm> (April 14, 2006).

2. Ibid.

3. Lamont Wood, "Battle of the Alamo: Introduction," *Heart of Texas,* 1999, <http:// hotx.com/alamo/intro.html> (April 14, 2006).

4. William Barret Travis, as recited in a speech by Senator Kay Bailey Hutchinson, "170th Anniversary of Texas Independence Day," *Congressional Record,* March 2, 2006, <http:// www.senate.gov/~hutchison/speec488.htm> (April 14, 2006).

Chapter 3. Revolution

1. Richard Bruce Winders, *Sacrificed at the Alamo: Tragedy and Triumph in the Texas Revolution* (Abilene, Tex.: State House Press, 2004), p. 17.

2. Ibid., p. 19.

Chapter 4. The People

1. Stephen L. Hardin, "Alamo, Battle of the," *The Handbook of Texas Online,* July 20, 2001, <http://www.tsha.utexas.edu/handbook/online /articles/AA/qeq2.html> (July 17, 2006).

2. James Atkins Shackford, *David Crockett: The Man and the Legend* (Chapel Hill: The University of North Carolina Press, 1956), pp. 211, 215.

3. William R. Williamson, "Bowie, Rezin Pleasant," *The Handbook of Texas Online,* June 6, 2001, <http://www.tsha.utexas.edu/handbook /online/articles/BB/fbo46.html> (July 17, 2006).

Chapter 5. Cannon and Sacrifice

1. Lamont Wood, "William Barret Travis," *Heart of Texas,* 1999, <http://www.hotx.com/ alamo/travis.html> (April 14, 2006).

2. Richard Bruce Winders, "General Orders of the 5th of March, 1836," from *Sacrificed at the Alamo: Tragedy and Triumph in the Texas Revolution* (Abilene, Tex.: State House Press, 2004) p. 122.

3. James Atkins Shackford, *David Crockett: The Man and the Legend* (Chapel Hill: The University of North Carolina Press, 1956), pp. 238–239.

4. Nolan Thompson, "Joe," *The Handbook of Texas Online,* June 6, 2001, <http://www.tsha .utexas.edu/handbook/online/articles/JJ/fjo1 .html> (July 17, 2006).

Chapter 6. Texas Independence and Statehood

1. Richard Bruce Winders, *Sacrificed at the Alamo: Tragedy and Triumph in the Texas Revolution* (Abilene, Tex.: State House Press, 2004), p. 133.

2. San Jacinto Monument and Museum of History, "The Battle of San Jacinto: April 21, 1836," *Sam Houston Area Council Boy Scouts of America,* n.d., <http://www.shac.org/Home /Forms/SanJacintoBattle/> (July 17, 2006).

Bankson, John. *Antonio López de Santa Anna*. Bear, Del.: Mitchell Lane Publishers, 2004.

Burgan, Michael. *The Alamo*. Minneapolis, Minn.: Compass Point Books, 2001.

Burke, Rick. *Davy Crockett*. Chicago: Heinemann Library, 2004.

Caravantes, Peggy. *An American in Texas: The Story of Sam Houston*. Greensboro, N.C.: Morgan Reynolds Publishing, 2004.

Coleman, Wim and Pat Perrin. *The Alamo: A MyReportLinks.com Book*. Berkeley Heights, N.J.: Enslow Publishers, Inc., 2005.

Gaines, Ann. *The Alamo: The Fight Over Texas*. Chanhassen, Minn.: Child's World, 2003.

Gaines, Ann Graham. *Jim Bowie: Hero of the Alamo*. Springfield, N.J.: Enslow Publishers, Inc., 2000.

Gregson, Susan R. *Sam Houston: Texas Hero*. Minneapolis, Minn.: Compass Point Books, 2006.

Murphy, Jim. *Inside the Alamo*. New York: Delacorte Press, 2003.

Nelson, Sheila. *A Proud and Isolated Nation: Americans Take a Stand in Texas*. Philadelphia: Mason Crest Publishers, 2005.

Stacy, Lee. ed. *Mexico and the United States*. New York: Marshall Cavendish, 2002.

Wade, Mary Dodson. *Texas History*. Chicago: Heinemann Library, 2004.